Images of Māori Women

Images of Māori Women

MATAAHUA WĀHINE

MICHELLE MOIR

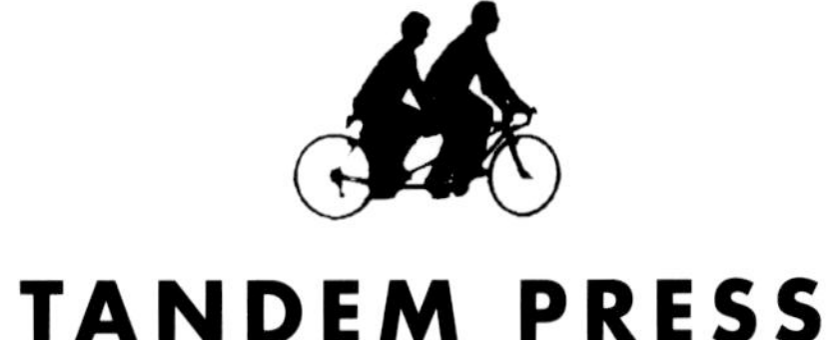

TANDEM PRESS

To Anne and Bob Moir
and all the women who appear in this book

First published in 1994 by
TANDEM PRESS
2 Rugby Road, Birkenhead, Auckland 10
New Zealand

ISBN 0-908884-49-4

Design and production by Pressgang, 17 Sale Street, Auckland.

Printed in Hong Kong by Everbest Printing Co. Ltd.

Contents

Me nekeneke!
Me nukunuku!
Neke ki tai, nuku ki tua
Ki ngā rerenga maha
Ngā whatinga o koutou
E kui, e kui, e kui mā!
Koutou nei ngā kanohi ora
Ngā piringa, ngā pānga
Ki a rātou te manomano.
Na, ka tuoho ka rere ngā mihi!

They stir!
They move!
They look seaward and
They look inland.
Seeking the elusive links
The fractured chains.
Yours are the living faces
That shelter, that embrace
The many of the past and the present.
You, the tau! the kōkā! the kuia!
We honour and greet you.

MERIMERI PENFOLD

Foreword

GLYNNIS PARAHA

In this book a Māori whakatauākī (proverb), the concept of whakapapa (genealogy), the state of te reo Māori (language), the medium of photography, and specially chosen wāhine Māori (Māori women) living in the 1990s in Pakipaki, Wellsford, the Hokianga and Kawakawa—have all been brought together to forge a unique relationship.

The whakatauākī 'He pounamu kakano rua' suggests that a piece of greenstone can be viewed in more than one way. The same is the case for Māori women: this book, like an M.Ed. thesis I completed in 1993 bearing the same title, asserts that Māori women should be seen not only through the way in which we are usually represented (through the eyes of non-Māori), but in a manner that validates the way we see ourselves.

The concept of whakapapa is very much part of this process. Each woman in the book was given a chance to identify and present herself in relation to her own personal, physical, spiritual and genealogical landscape. And so it is we see her in her bed at Pakipaki, in her back garden beside her harakeke (flax) in Moerewa, or in her home at Waiomio with pictures of her children, grandchildren and great-grandchildren behind her. These are the places from which many wāhine Māori view the world (as opposed to the way many colonial artists and film-makers have viewed them); and in the process we learn who they are, where they stand, and the struggles each has encountered as a wahine Māori living in a Pākehā-dominated society.

One of the themes that recur in the captions is the corporal punishment many experienced at school for speaking te reo Māori instead of English. Mere Tuhi Wilson vividly describes how she gradually lost confidence in using the language, Wyna Kathryn Monica Rowe speaks of the feelings of inadequacy of Māori people who cannot converse in their own language, and Kelly Anne Marie Jessup tells us that she has become involved at her local Kohanga Reo (language nest) in Pakipaki because 'children who attend grow and develop in a manner that was denied their parents and grandparents'.

When these photographic images, accompanied by unconventionally long, often heartfelt captions in both te reo Maori and English, were finally exhibited at Te Taumata Gallery, my kuia, aunts, cousins and nieces made the trip from Kawakawa and Pakipaki. After the powhiri (welcome), each began vying for viewing space. Soon exclamations of 'See this kuia of yours . . . well, her youngest sister married my . . . ' began to be heard. From the long-held embraces and subsequent, soft 'oohs' and 'aahs' that echoed round the small gallery, it was obvious that whakapapa had begun to weave its magic.

From the beginning, while working on this project, Michelle and her Rolliflex camera were accompanied to each woman's kainga (home) by someone the woman knew and trusted. Michelle came to learn about the realities in which these women lived, their cultural allegiances and experiences, and at all times she maintained the position of manuhiri (visitor), which implies that entry into these women's lives was a privilege.

My interest in visual media, including photography, and the focus of my research was nurtured by twelve years of living, teaching, and travelling in Europe, America and Scandinavia, experiencing cultures that had been overpowered by colonising forces, just as my own had been—the Algerians by the French, the Icelanders by the Swedes, the Norwegians and Greenlanders by the Danes, and the Native Americans by European colonialists. At the bottom of each social pile I met indigenous women, marginalised by a colonising power, who were fighting for their identity.

These photographic images are a collaborative effort on the part of the many Māori women who became involved. It is important to acknowledge that neither Michelle's photographs, nor my thesis, nor the current travelling exhibition and the publication of this book could have been undertaken without the support and encouragement of many kuia. Their respected presence in my life, and within the confines of these covers, remains the catalyst for pursuing my research in the same area.

In Māori society the voice of the woman is the first that is heard on any marae. No formal hui can proceed without that call. This book asserts the oral traditions and systems of Māori women and refutes the way in which they appear—invisible and voiceless—in Pākehā literary and visual traditions. Instead, now is the time to celebrate the mana, the ihi, the wehi, the mauri and the wairua of wāhine Māori; for I believe, like my friend Linda Smith, that 'the time for us to fit ourselves into someone else's reflection is over'.

Preface

MICHELLE MOIR

During 1992 I travelled to many parts of the North Island, from the Hawke's Bay to the Hokianga, to spend time with Māori women, young and old, in their own homes. Using a Rolliflex camera I photographed each woman in her own landscape, and in turn each woman wrote a piece about herself to accompany her image.

This book represents months of travelling, photographing, living with families, and, most importantly, forming friendships with the women I was honoured to be introduced to.

To have been welcomed into these women's lives has been an experience that will always be part of me, and I would like to thank all of them for giving me the trust and support that allowed this work to evolve. I would also like to acknowledge the sad loss of Waina Ross during 1993.

A number of women have made this work possible:

Firstly, I would like to thank Glynnis Paraha for sharing with me her thesis work on 'Images of Māori Women' and for introducing me to her whānau in Pakipaki, Hawke's Bay, where this series of portraits began and grew.

Thank you also to Wyna Rowe for her great hospitality and support in Pakipaki. This hospitality and support was continued throughout my work by Helene Leaf and Nicole Presland in the Hokianga, Rubina Strongman in Kawakawa, Waina Billington in Leigh, and Carol Ashby in Wellsford. My warmest thanks to each one of you for all your assistance.

I extend a most sincere thank you to Merimeri Penfold for her patience and for her tremendous help with the preparation of the text while I was at Elam School of Fine Arts, University of Auckland, working on this project.

I also thank Annais Allen and Janine McVeagh of Te Reo Publications for their wholehearted support and continual encouragement. Their involvement with this book has been an essential ingredient, and I appreciate immensely the energy that they have both given to this project, especially the editing of the text.

I also extend a warm thank you to Helen Benton and Bob Ross of Tandem Press for publishing this book and making it accessible to many.

Kellie Anne Marie Jessup

PAKIPAKI

Ko Kahuranaki te maunga.
Ko Ngaruroro te awa.
Ko Takitimu te waka.
Ko Ngāti Rangikoianake rāua ko Mihiroa aku hapu.
Ko Ngāti Kahungunu te iwi.

Ko Hori Tupaea rāua ko Kereni Bartlett ōku mātua.
Ko Eunice Kay rāua ko Clifford Miles ōku mātua whāngai.

Ko ahau te kaiako o Te Kupenga a Te Huki Te Kohanga Reo Pakipaki, Taraia Marae.

Ko Kohanga Reo te taonga o ngā tamariki katoa.
E tipu e rea.

The Kohanga Reo is the treasure of all children.

I was born and bred in Hastings, attending Frimley Primary School, Heretaunga Intermediate and Hastings Girls High School. I married when I was twenty-one and had three children. My husband, Larry Jessup, is of Kahungunu descent.

After helping my mother, Kereni Bartlett, founder of this Kohanga Reo, as a kaiawhina, I reluctantly took over as kaiako when the second kaiako, Mrs Crete White, left to further her Māori studies at Teachers' Training College in Palmerston North.

Initially I felt that I was not qualified enough to take over, but I have since learnt to overcome all my insecurities and lack of confidence in myself. I began with my own study of Māoritanga and tikanga. With all the trials and tribulations this position introduces, I have found a stronger, more confident and more understanding person within myself.

Kohanga Reo is of great significance for Māori. It is essential in the all-round development of our tamariki. I am proud to be a part of it all.

I can remember as a child—how shy, reserved and withdrawn I was. With the introduction of Kohanga Reo, Māori children who attend are able to grow and develop in a manner that was denied their parents and grandparents.

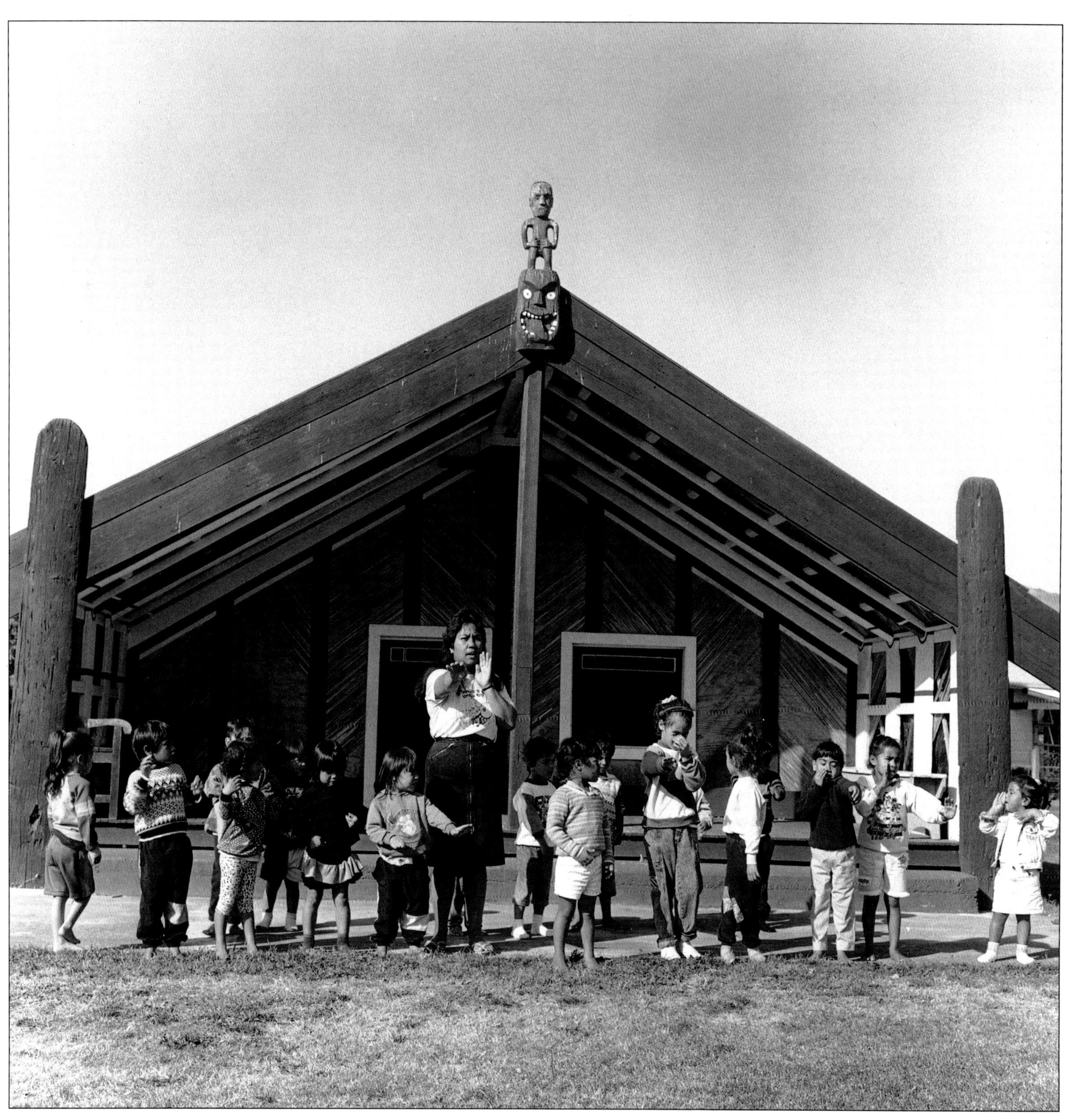

Rikirangi Hawaikirangi

OPAPA

Ko Kahungunu te iwi.
Ko Ngāti Whatuiāpiti te hapu.
Ko te Kikiri me Rangitāne ngā hapu.

I grew up in Te Hauke and have never gone away to work. I am the great-great-granddaughter of Te Hapuku. I was the fifth of thirteen, born on 22 April 1909.

I went to Te Hauke Missionary School and then Opapa Primary School in 1918. I had the strap twice for speaking Māori at school. They used to think we were swearing and would rinse our mouths out with soap.

I married Tiopira Hape when I was eighteen and we had six children. After he died I married Petera Whakahoro Rapihana Hawaikirangi, a carpenter and farmer.

Our days began at four a.m. with hand-milking a hundred and twenty cows, and ended after tea and bathing, with all the chores of a busy household in between. On Saturdays everyone helped with the farm work. Sunday was family day.

Everyone dressed in their best clothes and went to church; after church we came home to the big traditional Sunday lunch—roast lamb with all the trimmings.

We all looked forward to Sunday.

I am blessed with my six children, twenty-one grandchildren, forty-two great-grandchildren, and one great-great-grandchild.

I never talk Māori to my grandkids, because they don't know what I'm saying.

When my grandchildren attended colleges around New Zealand and I visited them, I was adopted by my grandchildren's friends and became Nanny to many children.

The happiest time for me is when my whānau come to visit. But I am very sad, a 'howl bag' or 'tangiweto' when the time comes for them to go back to their homes or jobs.

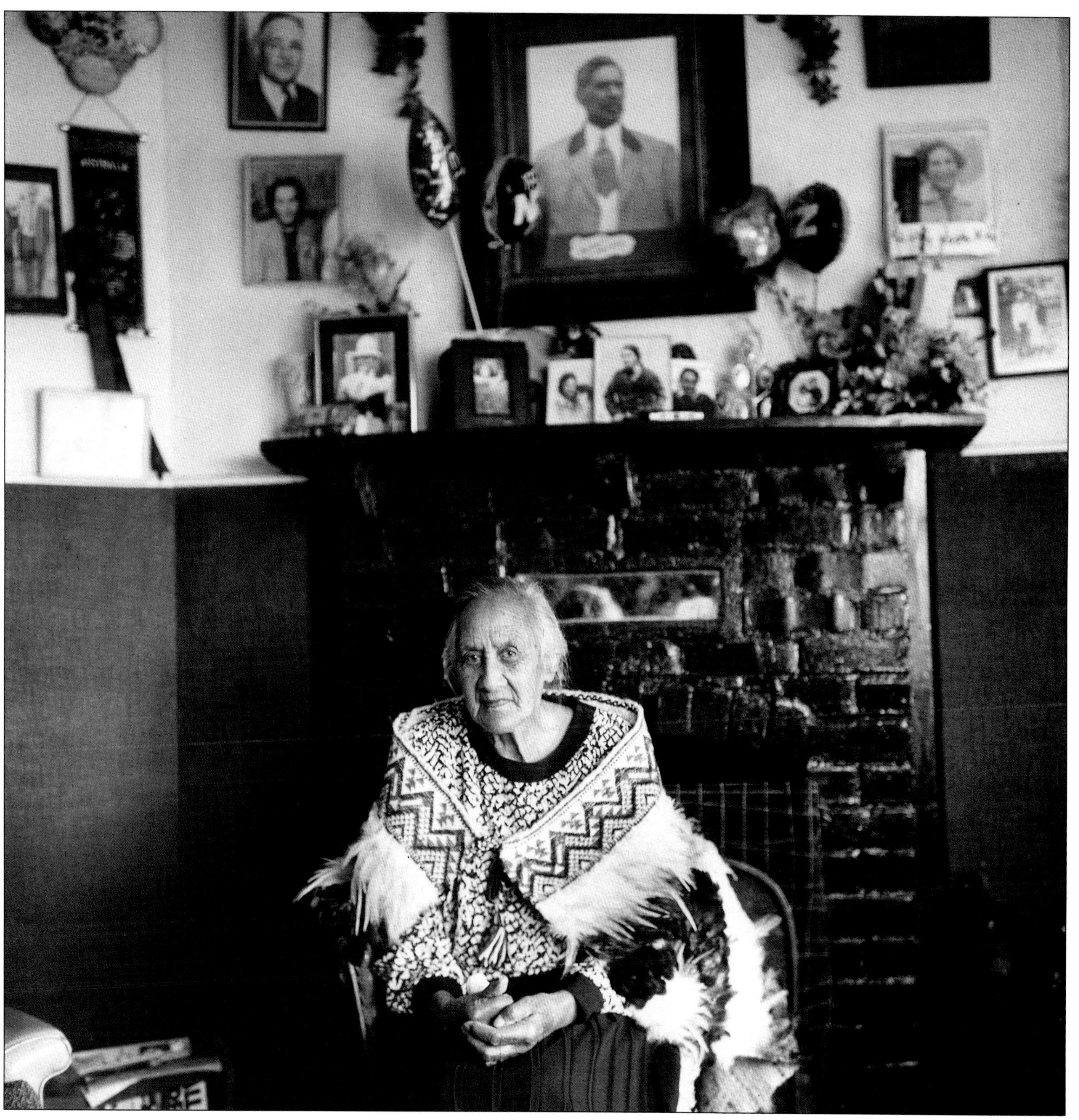

Tanira Hemana Te Rohu Te Au

PAKIPAKI

Ko Ngāti Kahungunu te iwi.
Ko Papatumaro te hapu.
Ko Ngarengare te hapu.

I perceive myself as going through the system in education, work situations, and family life, raising children and then returning to the family marae at Pakipaki, and discovering an awakening of feelings that here are my roots, my heritage.

Now I am content to be at home, bringing up a mokopuna, Heather, as my own child. There is a completeness—a fulfilment—in my life.

To me, this is what being Māori is about—embracing and loving our own, and bringing together all that is life.

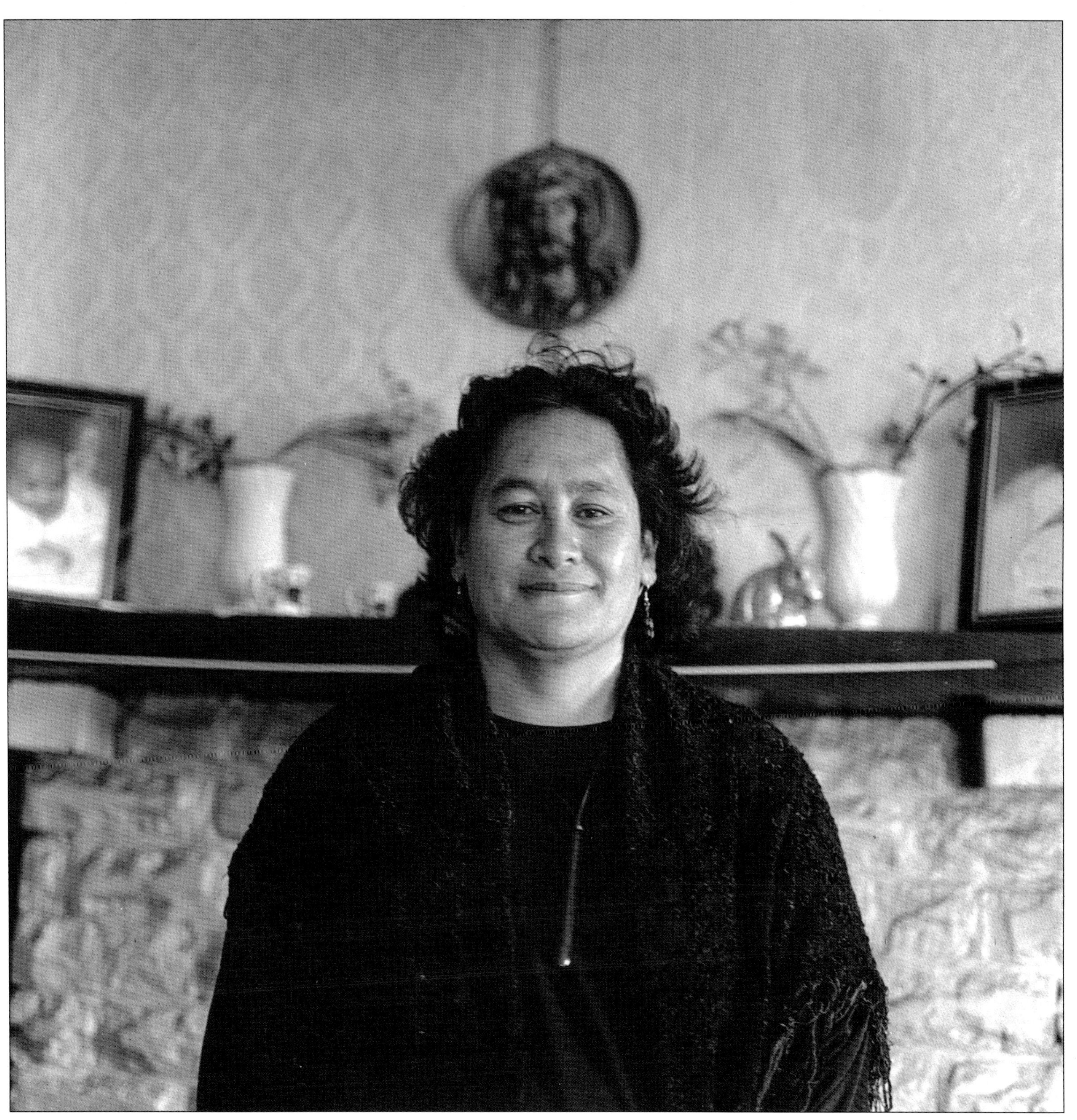

Maraea Nia Nia-Yates

NAPIER

Ko Whakapunaki te maunga.
Ko Ruakituri me Hangaroa-a-huri-noa-ki-te-kaitarahae ngā awa.
Ko Te Reinga te marae.
Ko Hinekorako te taniwha.
Ko Ngāti Hinehika te hapu.
Ko Ngāti Kahungunu te iwi.

Kaiako: Te Wharetangata.

My early childhood was spent with my koro and kuia, who influenced greatly the direction my life took. I travelled with them to all the Ringatu hui they attended throughout the North Island, and so today I am involved in Māori initiatives, particularly in the field of health.

At present I am involved with the local cervical screening programme.

Māori women for me are like Papatūānuku, providing life, nourishment and sustenance for their people. Māori women play an important role within the community and have been to the fore for many years, culturally, socially and politically.

I see for myself more involvement at all levels of health initiatives so that we as Māori find services more appropriate and sensitive to our needs.

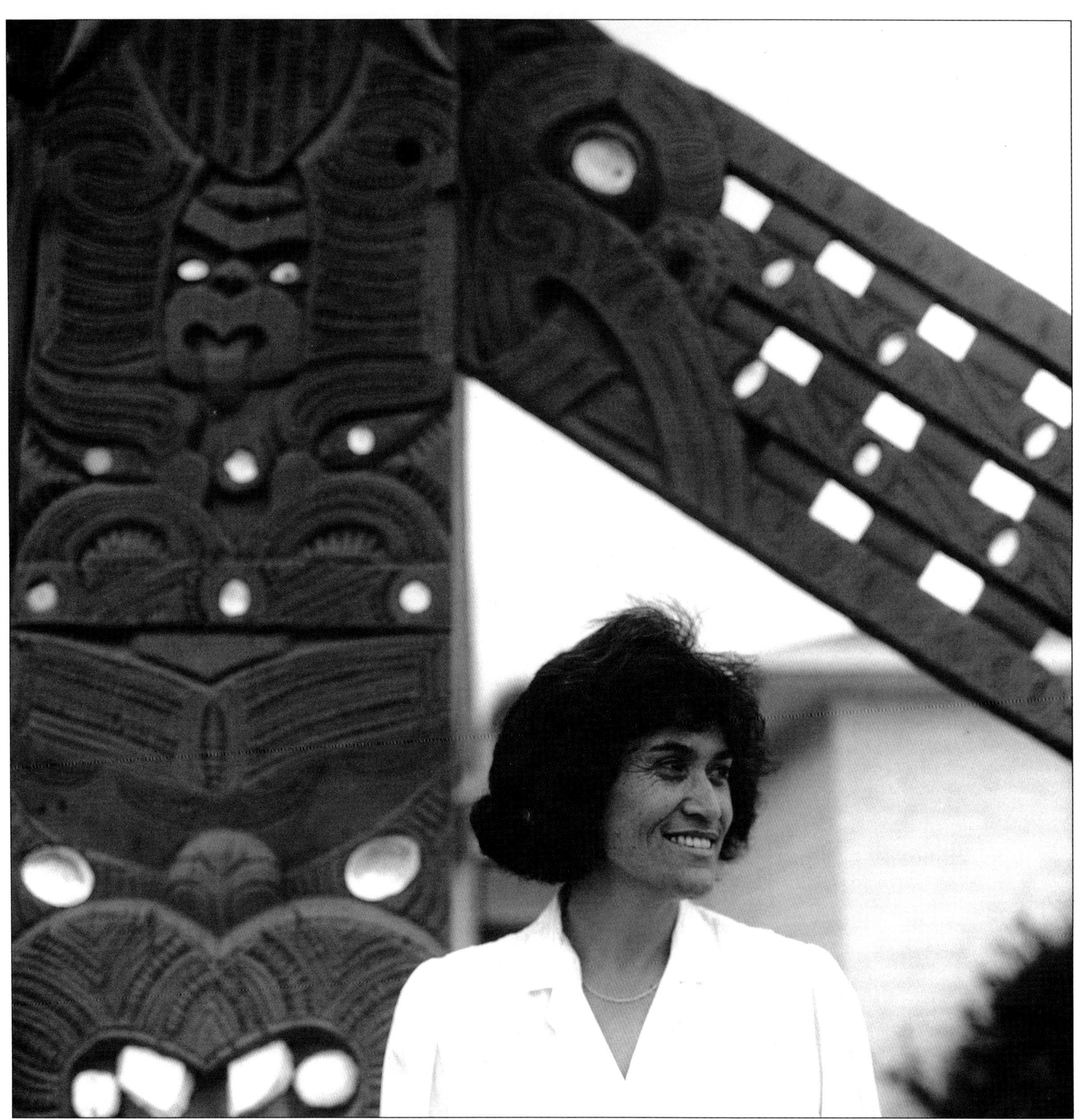

Mere Tuhi Wirihana

OPAPA

Ko Ngāti Whakiti Kahungunu te iwi.

My mother was Tahuri Hera Edwards, and my father was Fred Burgess. My mother was full Māori and couldn't speak a word of English. My father was European. I was born in 1902.

In 1914 I went to Hukarere College in Napier. The punishment at school for speaking Māori was severe. We would write thousands of lines saying, 'I will not speak Māori.'

I finished college in 1918 and did all sorts of jobs.

I married Nia Nia Wirihana in 1931. In our married life we had one of the biggest shearing contracts in Hawke's Bay. I did wool-classing too. We had the contract for forty years. Then Nia Nia passed away and I retired.

I live the Māori way, but I've lost some of the Māori language. I miss words in sentences and have to stop and think.

I worked on this marae to get a dining room—we were the first around here to build one. I said to them, 'I don't want presents for my ninetieth birthday, but will they donate something to our marae.'

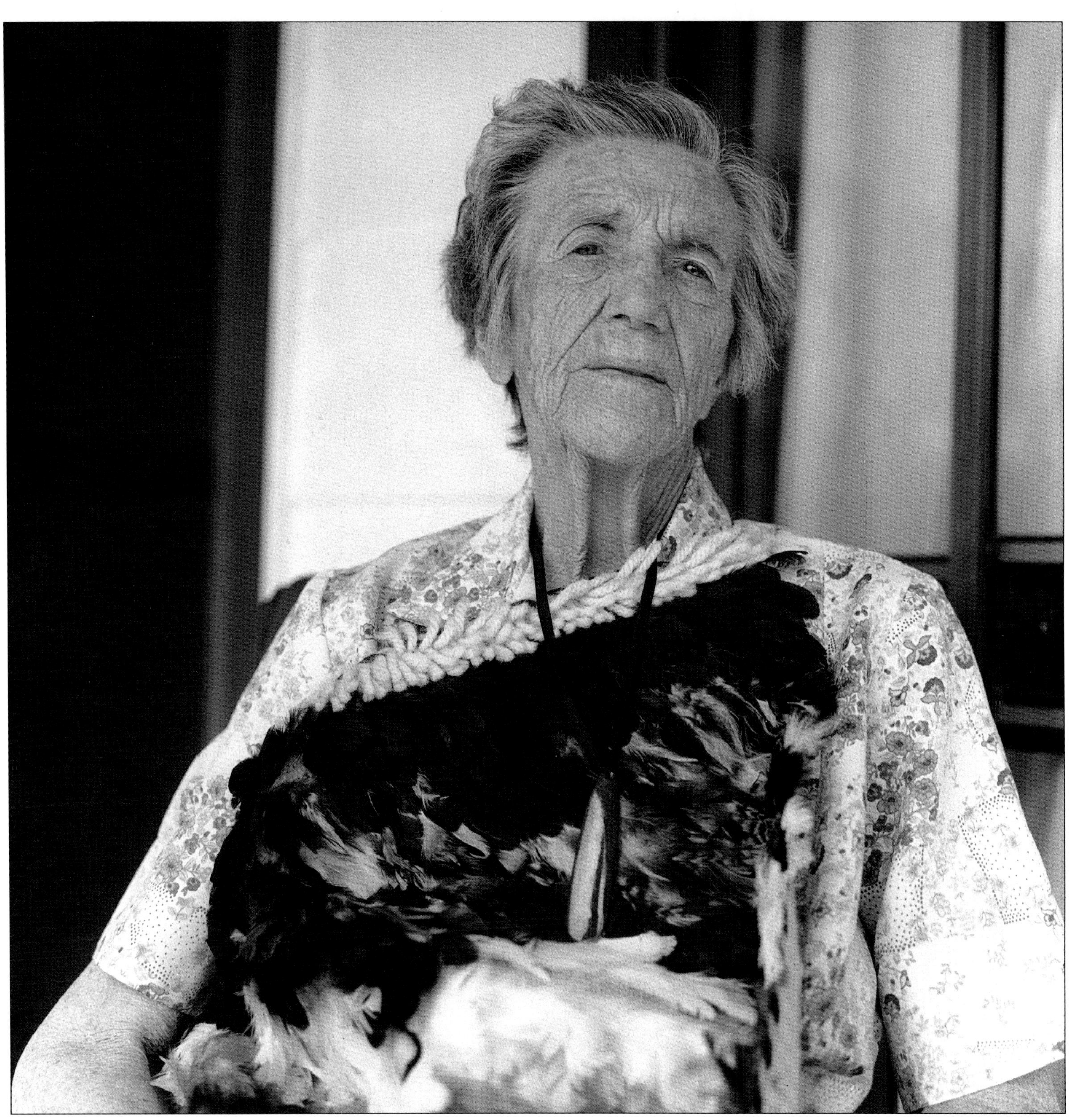

Maria Merehinekete Gerbes

HAVELOCK NORTH

Ko Kahungunu ki Heretaunga te iwi.
Ko Ngāti Ngarengare te hapu.

I am company secretary for my husband's business, Gunac H.B. (1968) Ltd, where I do accounts for our companies here in Hastings and in Christchurch. I use a computer involving all facets and stages of accounts payable, accounts receivable, payroll and general ledger—i.e. financial accounts for both companies.

I perceive myself as an ordinary person using the abilities I have to improve my son's and daughters' futures.

My work enables me to help provide a better standard of life for my family. It also gives hope to other Māori women—that if she (I) can do it, there must be hope for them.

I maintain that examples in life always assist people in their way of thinking and doing things, whether positive or negative.

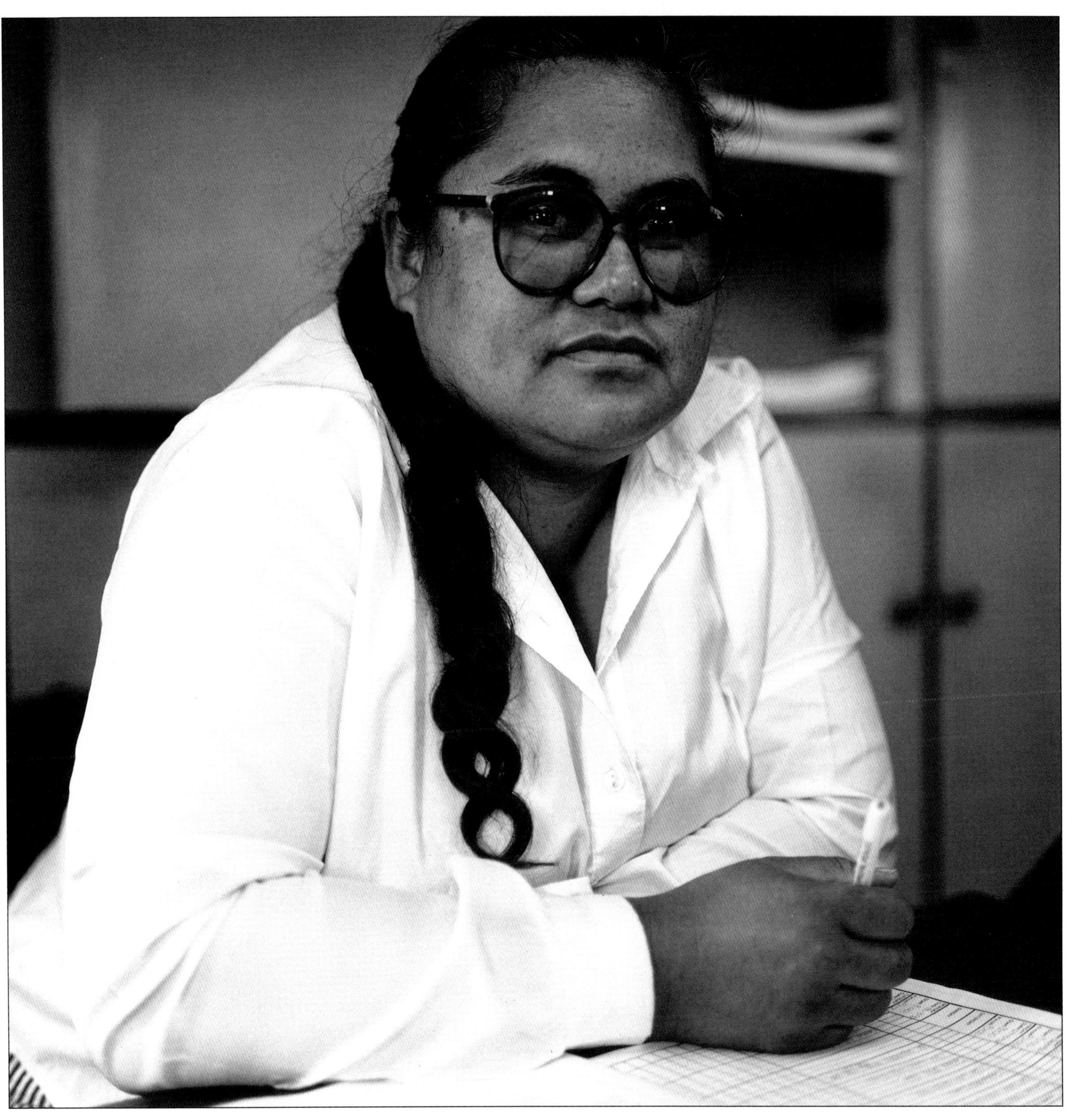

MARIA MEREHINEKETE GERBES

Helen Hape

TE HAUKE

Takitimu te waka.
Kahungunu te iwi.
Kahuranaki te maunga.
Poukawa te wai.
Te Whatuiāpiti te hapu.
Te Rangikoianake te Tangata.
Kahuranaki, Keke, Te Whatuiāpiti ngā marae.

I was born in 1941 at Waipawa, which is thirty miles to the south of Pakipaki. My mother was born at Te Hauke, and my father was born at Kairakau. I come from a family of seventeen brothers and sisters.

When our mother died in 1957, I was the oldest at home, so I left school to take care of my younger brothers and sisters, as my father said we would all end up in a home.

My first job was at Wattie's cannery in Hastings. I met and married my first husband, Sonny Tahatuoterangi Otene, and we had three sons: Ashley Karaitiana, Lester Tahatuoterangi and Leon Lane.

My second husband, Colin Hape, and I have a daughter, Coline Rikirangi.

I became very active in my children's education, beginning with playcentre and continuing through to high school. With my daughter, especially, I was very involved with her high school—PTA, board of governors, library.

I can honestly say I was being educated with my children, right up until today. The individuals I have met over the years through my children's schooling have been an education in themselves.

My mokopuna are as important a part of me as this place where I live. They are: Te Whatuiapiti, aged ten, Jahna, aged four, Noema Tamahine, aged two, and Ashley Amy Te Whetu, aged seven months.

For the future, while taking care of Ashley Amy Te Whetu, I'll attend the local kohanga with her and have myself and my moko speaking Māori.

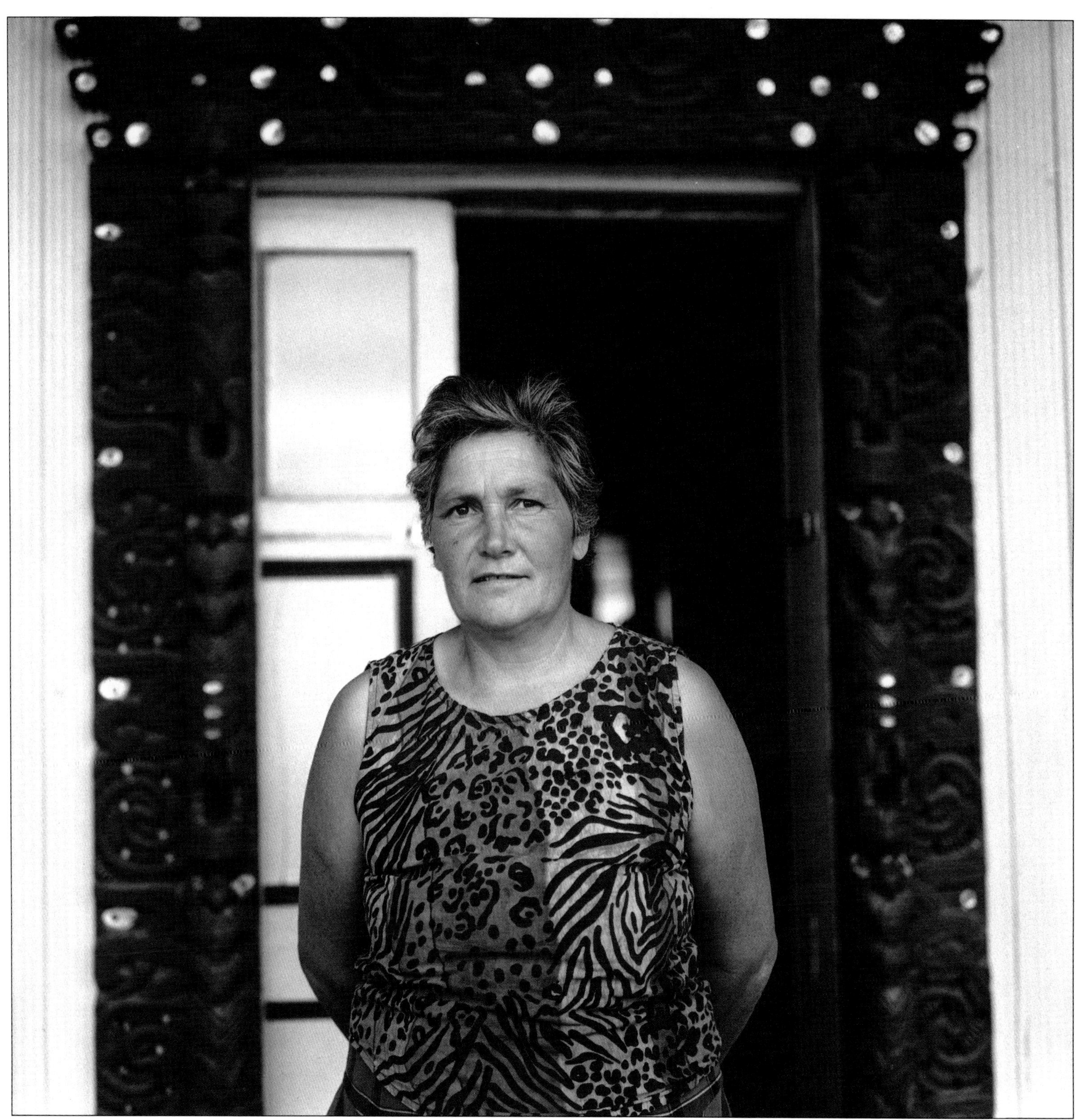

Waiata McClutchie

PAKIPAKI

Ko Ngāti Kahungunu ki Heretaunga, Atiawa, Ngai Tahu ngā iwi.
Ko Ngāti Whatuiāpiti, ko Papatuamaroa ngā hapu.
Ko Takitimu te waka.

My parents were Matahaere Hararutu Russell and James Tiemi Lyon Russell. My grandparents were Riripeti Minhinnick (Atiawa) and Te Taite (Ngāti Kahungunu ki Heretaunga).

I was born in Greytown but brought up by my Auntie Putiputi Nihera Timu at Poukawa, between Pakipaki and Te Hauke, where I have lived most of my life.

My mother and auntie were well known for the poi, and my father was well known for the haka and was actively involved with Houngarea Marae at Pakipaki. In my younger years, I helped to compose Māori songs with Waimarama Puhara, a chief of Pakipaki. I gave the tunes; he gave the words. One of our songs was 'E Koro e te Huki'.

I was educated at Poukawa and Pakipaki Schools. After leaving school I worked with my parents on shearing contracts around Hawke's Bay and learnt to be a wool-classer. I also worked at Wattie's cannery for years.

I married Dave McClutchie from Ngāti Porou and had six children and a foster-daughter. So far I have thirty-three grandchildren and twenty-eight great-grandchildren.

Although I spent my married life in Hastings, my greatest wish was to return to my roots in Pakipaki.

I am now seventy-five years old. I have been a resident at the Kakirawa Flats in Pakipaki for five years.

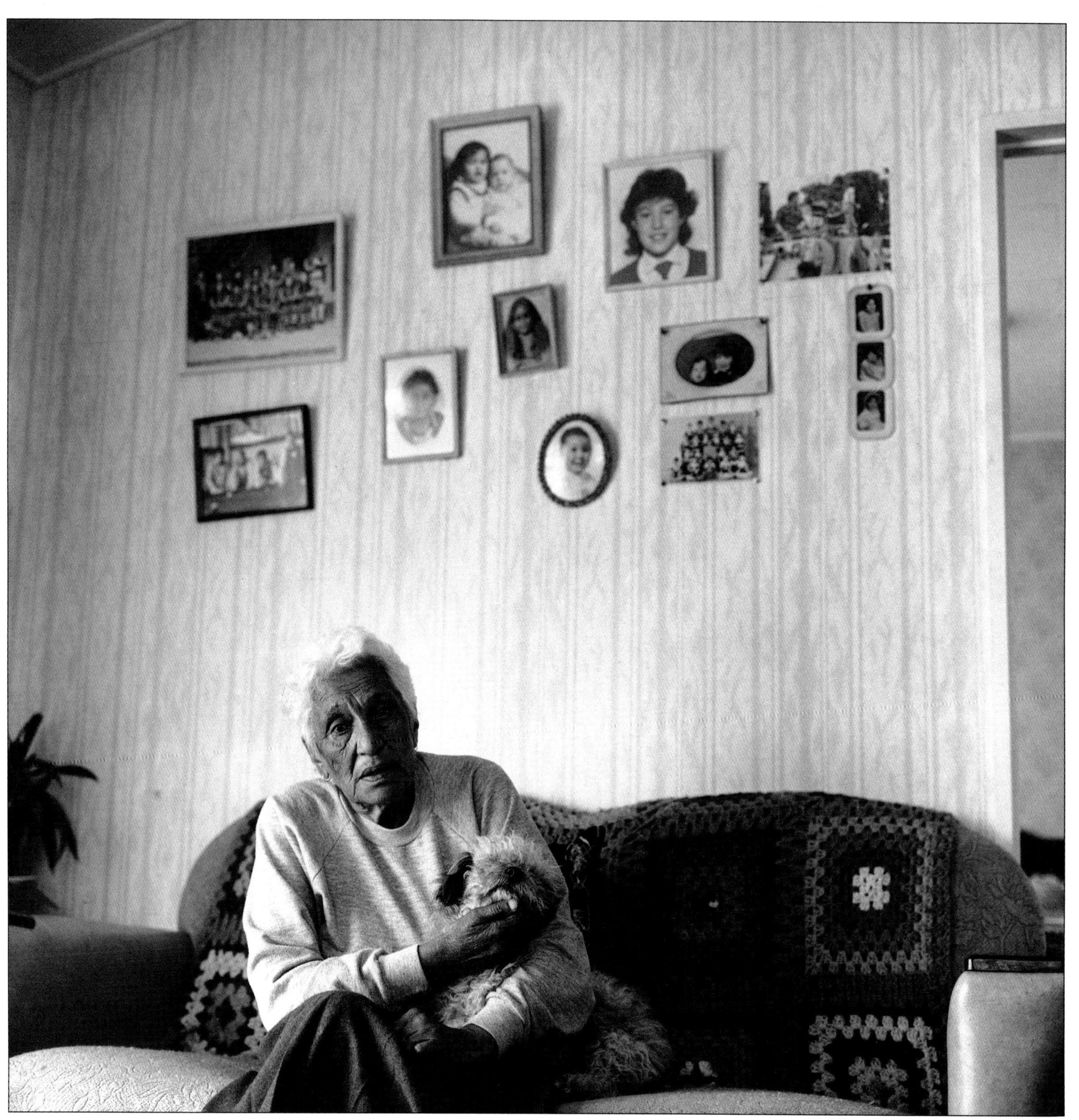

Wyna Kathryn Monica Rowe

PAKIPAKI

Ko Kahungunu ki Heretaunga te iwi.
Ko Ngarengare te hapu.
Ko Kahuranaki te maunga.
Ko Ngaruroro te awa.

Myself! Looking back at my earlier days as a Māori girl, I feel a sense of loss, in respect that at no time during my school days was there any Māoritanga or culture taught, and because it was also forbidden in my parents' era to speak their native tongue in front of me or my other sisters and brothers.

But today the school system now allows, whether you're Māori or of any other race, to learn the Māoritanga, culture and heritage at preschool age and to go on through high school and university.

I feel a great sense of loss, and now at the age of thirty-six I am striving to rectify the injustice done to me, by learning myself, and encouraging my children. We can stand tall and be proud of being Māori and the heritage we are so lucky to be part of.

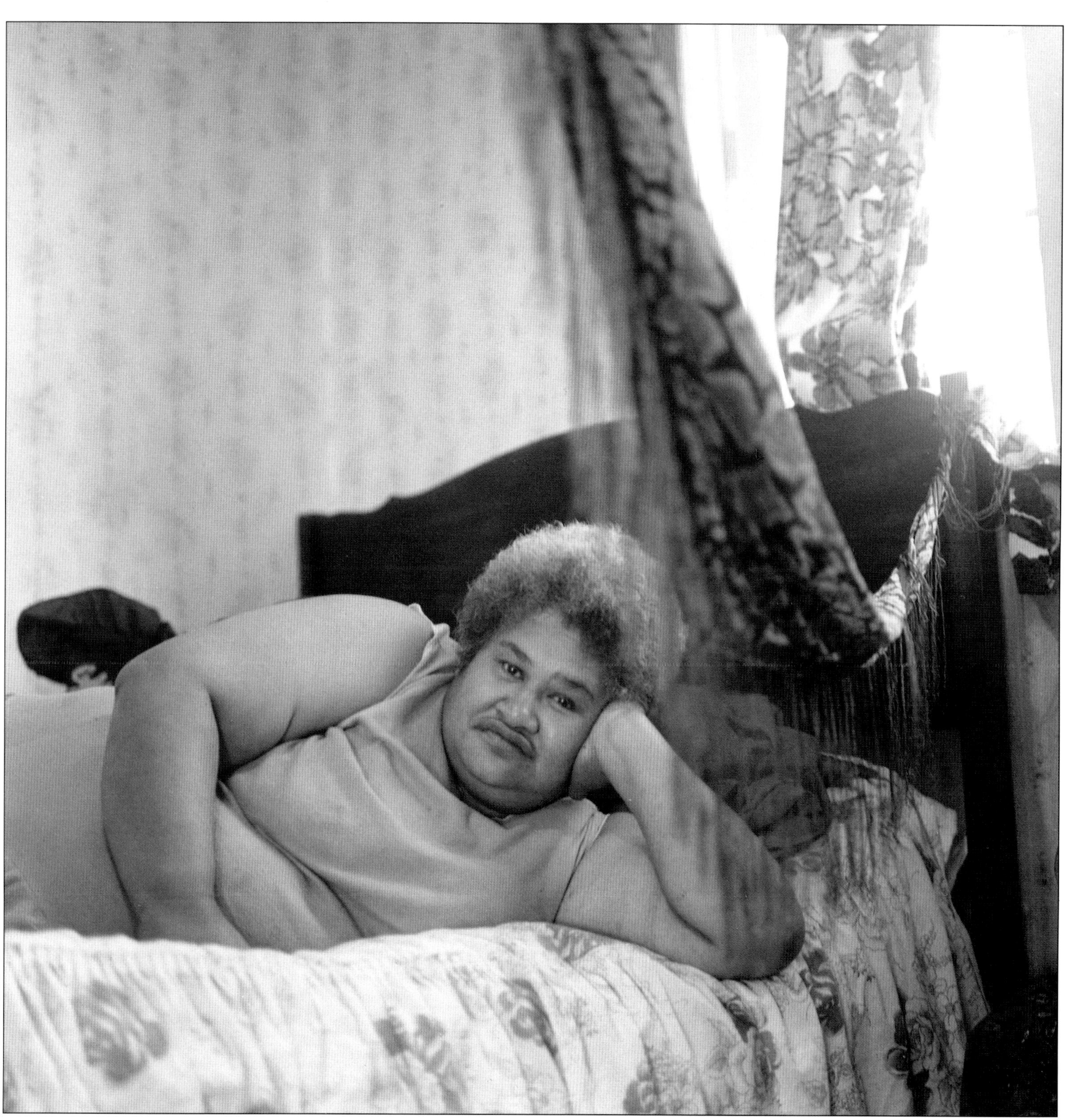

Hine Aroha Millward

PAKIPAKI

Ko Ngāti Haunui-a-paparangi te iwi.
Ko Ngāti Apa te hapu.
Ko Taranaki te maunga.
Ko Whanganui te awa.
Ko Aotea te waka.

My birthplace was Wanganui and my growing-up years were in various places. My early years of growing up were in Pakipaki until I was nine years of age, then in a little place called Greatford, near Bulls, and from there to Eketahuna in the Wairarapa, where I finished my schooling.

At the age of seventeen years I worked at Napier Public Hospital, and married my first husband while living in Napier. I remarried in 1977, to my second husband, and altogether have had eight children.

I now live in Pakipaki and am involved with Māori culture. During my growing-up years I knew nothing of Māoritanga or tikanga Māori, as most of my life I lived among the Europeans.

Learning about myself as a Māori has been the most wonderful thing that has happened for me. I now tutor Māori culture at Hastings Girls High School, which has given me a sense of worth for myself, and I feel very useful to our young people. Working with children and teenagers is a very satisfying and gratifying part of my life.

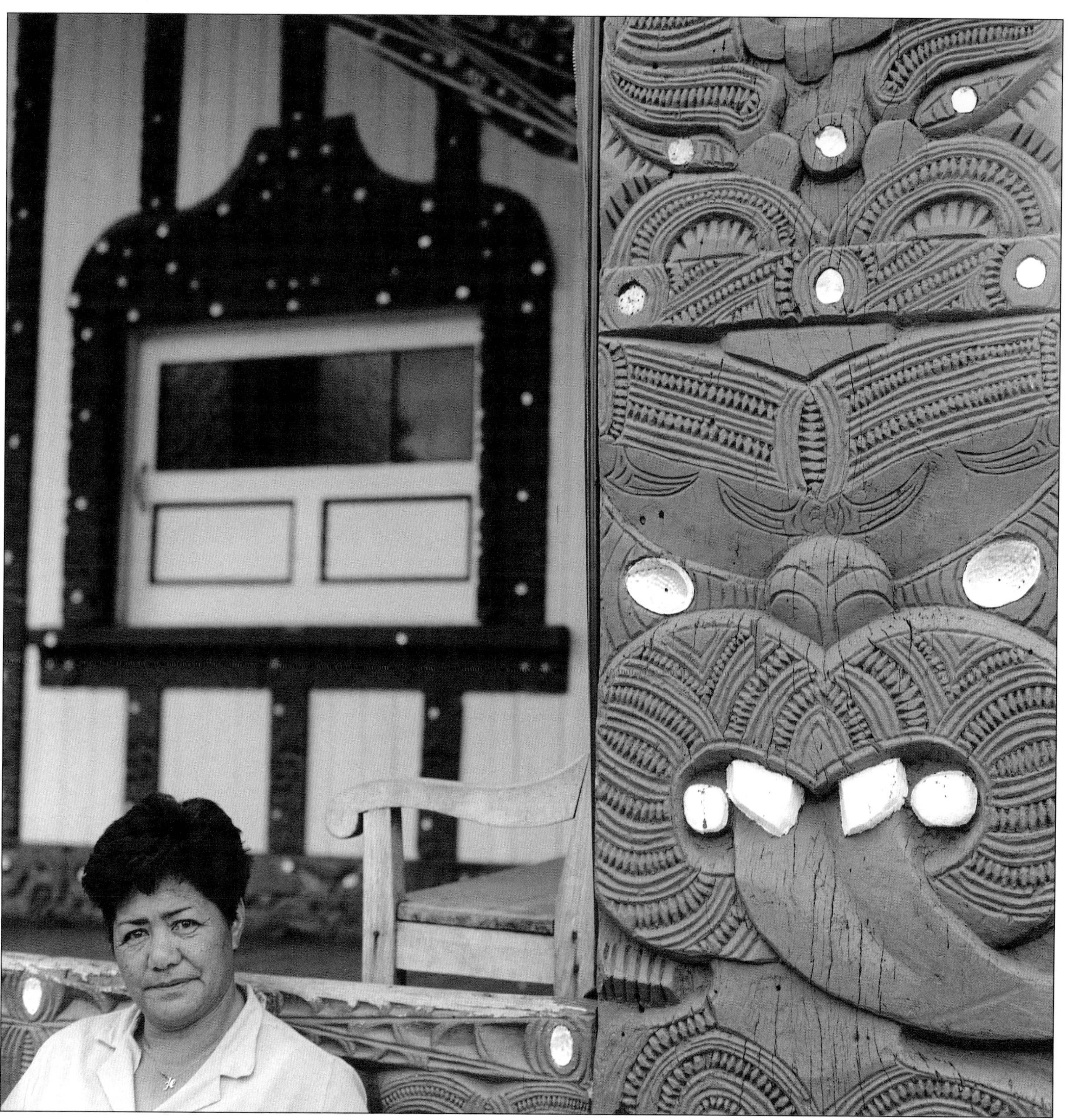

Merehira Taurerewa Rowe

PAKIPAKI

Ko Kahungunu ki Heretaunga te iwi.
Ko Ngarengare te hapu.
Ko Kahuranaki te maunga.
Ko Ngaruroro te awa.

Ko Jack Porokoru Urikore Taurerewa Rowe taku tāne. We were blessed with eight children—two boys and six girls. We raised them at Anderson Road, Pakipaki, where I still reside today with my youngest son.

I have represented Hawke's Bay in netball and hockey, and was runner-up in New Zealand darts. I represented Hastings in the ladies' doubles at the Fiji darts tournament, and travelled also to England in 1984.

My beloved husband passed away the same year (1984), and my daughter Rosemary joined him in February 1985.

I have worked at our three marae, Houngarea, Mihiroa and Taraia, as a masseur. I went to Rarotonga on a working holiday and worked at Poutama Kite Ora as a masseur, then returned to England for the 1991 Rugby World Cup. I stayed on for four months, visiting my son and his family in Coventry.

There were three boys and five girls in my family. My father, Wi Te Kani Hori, and my mother, Merehinekete Tangatake (Kani), taught me Māori tikanga and protocol. I have been and am still to this day a kaikaranga on our marae.

I love my families dearly and thank God for the life I have had and am still living.

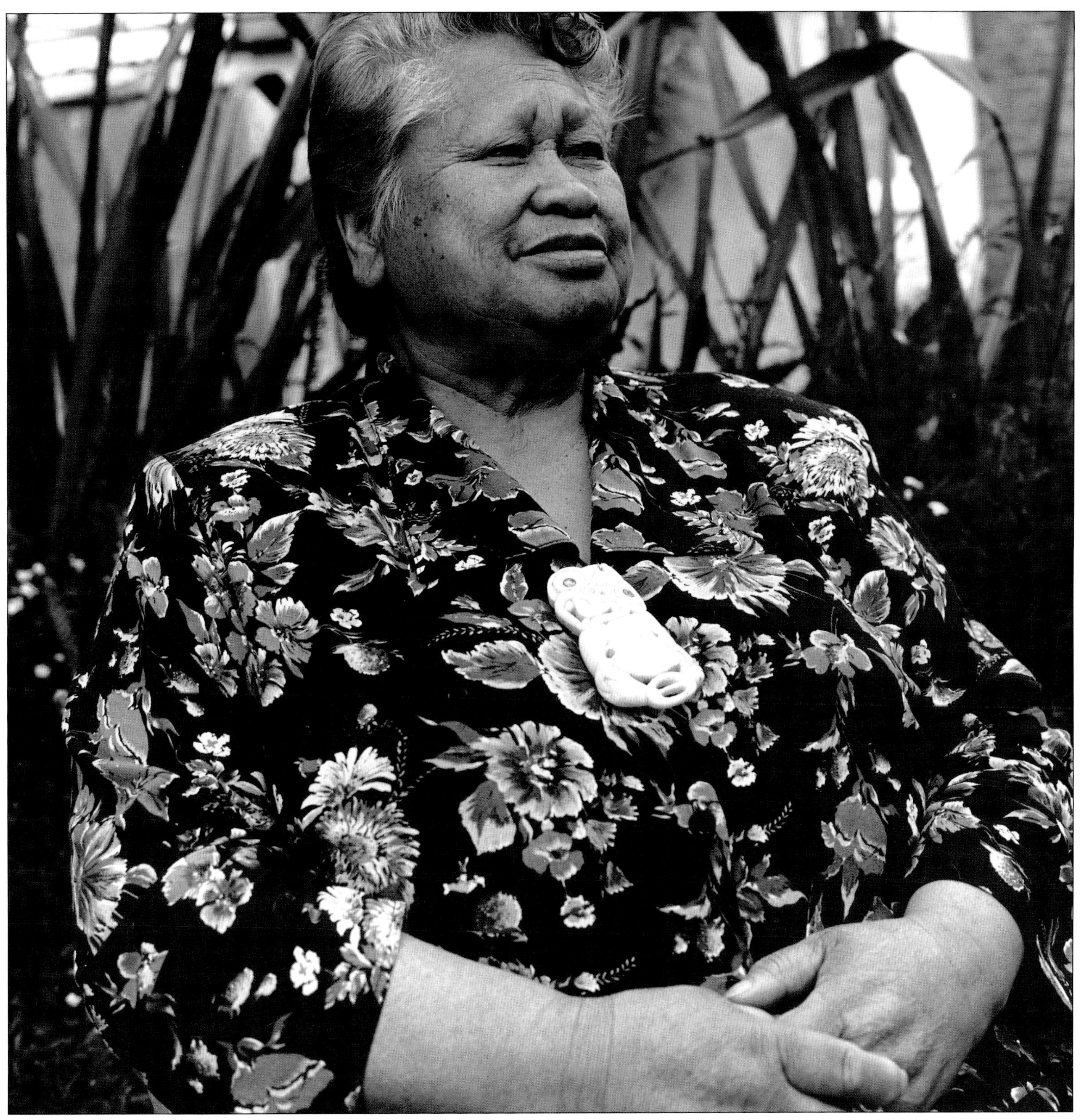

Lorraine Mihi Gray

NAPIER

Ko Ngāti Kahungunu te iwi.
Ko Ngāti Pahauwera me Ngāti-Upokoriri ngā hapu.

My reason for being at Houngarea Marae today was to assist with cervical screening of Māori women. I see myself taking this service to wherever—to a home, marae or clinic.

I was born and educated in Central Hawke's Bay, Waipawa, Tikokino and Central Hawke's Bay College.

I always wanted to be a nurse, but that didn't eventuate until I had married and had my family. As they were growing up I was nurse-aiding; then I wanted to go further, so I did my enrolled nurse's training and registered in 1980.

From there I have become involved with the changes in health, especially Māori health, and finding out how things could be made better for our people, particularly our Māori women and families.

I was involved with the National Council of Māori Nurses. We made changes in the nursing training for our people, so that nurses would be aware of the cultural needs when they moved into the health system.

My other involvement with community groups, such as the Māori Women's Welfare League, Māori Wardens and Victim Support, bring me in touch with our women and put me in a position to assist.

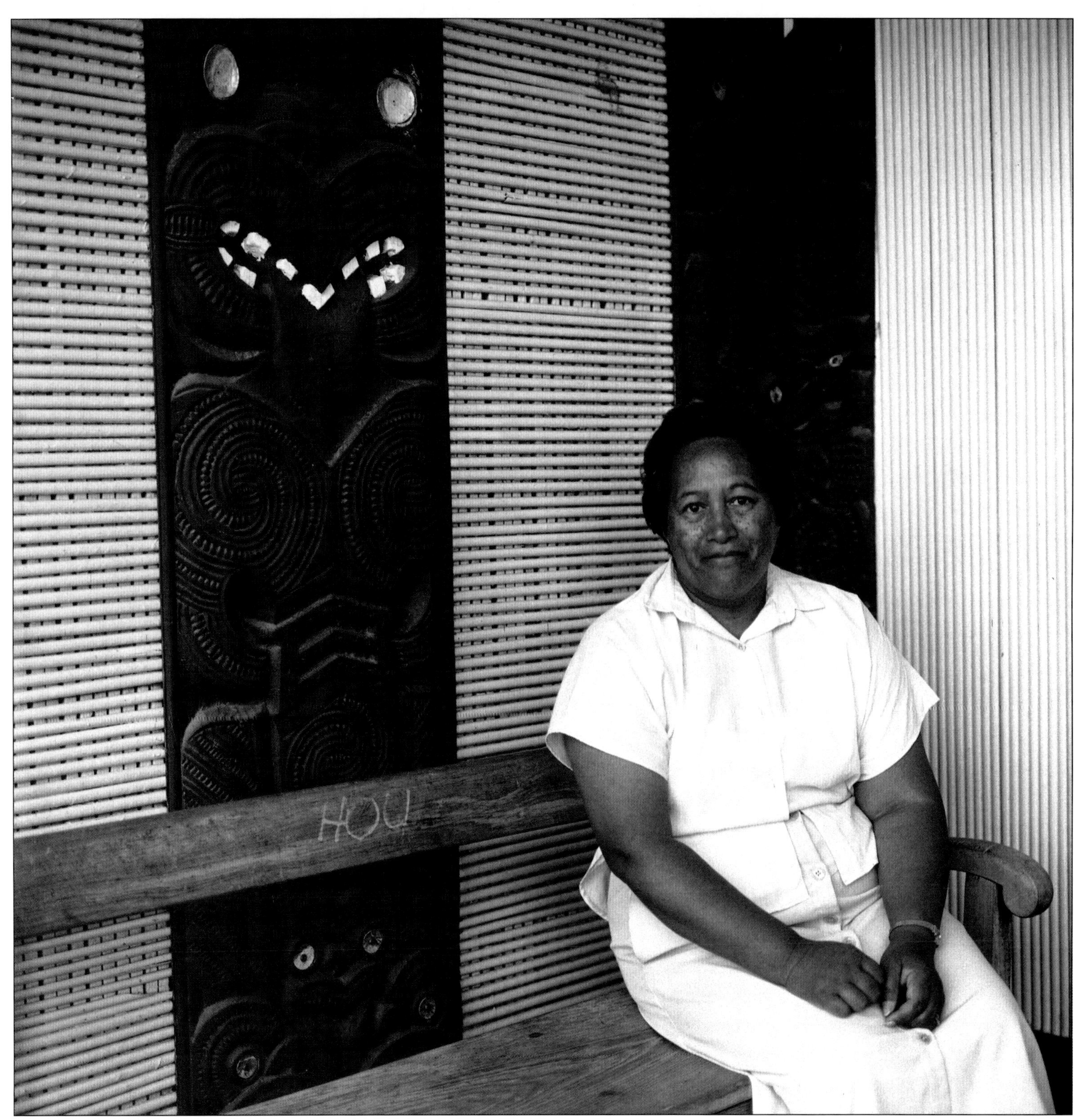

LORRAINE MIHI GRAY ▪

Katerina Minhinnick

WELLSFORD

Hikurangi te maunga.
Waiapu te awa.
Ngāti Porou te iwi.
Whānau-a-Apanui te hapu.
Kaiaio te marae.
Nukutere me Horouta ngā waka.
Kereu te awa iti.

Ko Katerina Minhinnick tōkū ingoa. Ko Hamiora Kemara rāua ko Mata Te Tawai āku mātua.

I whānau au i te tau 1938, ā, ko au te tokotoru o ngā pōtiki o te whānau. I kuraina ahau ki te kura tuatahi me te kura tuarua o Te Kaha. Me tono ahau ki te kura o Kuini Wikitoria i Akarana mai i te 1954–56.

Na, ka haere ahau hei kaiako ki te kura tuatahi o Whangaparāoa. Ko Hikitia Tukaki taku hoa māhita i reira. He tawhiti tonu atu tēnei kura i Te Kaha. Haere ai au ma runga i te taraka kawe kirīmi ki te wheketere o Te Kaha. He tino puehu te huarahi. I noho ahau ki te kainga o Rangaiti rāua ko Lucy Peta. He whanaunga nōku. He miraka kau ta rāua mahi i tāua wā.

I whakawhiti ahau ki Hanatere ki te kura Māori i Rākaumanga i roto i te rohe o ngā Kingitanga. I reira ka tutaki ahau ki taku hoa rangatira, David Minhinnick. Ko Hukanui tana kainga. Tainui te waka. Waikato te awa. Ngāti te Ata te iwi. I mārenatia māua e Canon Wite Tau Huata i te marae o Te Ohaki, i te tau kotahi mano, iwa rau, ono tekau—i ngā marama o Poutū-te-rangi.

Tokowhitu a māua tamariki—e rima ngā wāhine e rua ngā tāne. Tokowaru a māua mokopuna ināianei—e ono ngā tāne e rua ngā wāhine.

Koia nei te whakaahua o tā māua mokopuna a Wetere George Korito Minhinnick te whakapakanga o ā māua mokopuna.

Piki te kaha. Piki te ora. Te rangimarie ki ngā whānau katoa. Mā te Karaiti hei tautoko. Āke, Āke! Āmine!

I was born in the year 1938, and educated at Te Kaha MDHS, as it was known in those days. Two years at High School and then I was sent to Queen Victoria Māori Girls College in Parnell, 1954–56.

Back at Te Kaha I got a job as a junior assistant at Whangaparāoa School, Cape Runaway. Then I applied for a position as junior assistant at Rākaumanga Māori School, Huntly—among the Waikato people.

There I met David, and we married in 1960. After having a family of seven, five girls and two boys, I went as junior assistant at Oruawharo School, inland at Wellsford, from 1980 to 1982.

Kohanga Reo had started by then in Wellsford. In 1988 I was asked by the elders of Wellsford and Oruawharo if I would take on the position of kaiako at Te Puawaitanga me Ngā Hau e Wha (The Blossoming of the Four Winds) Kohanga Reo.

I accepted, and have been here since. It has been a very rewarding experience. It has helped to rekindle my ties with my Māori language and history.

At the moment my eight mokopuna keep me quite active. Wetere George Korito Minhinnick, who is in the photo with me, is the youngest one of my grandchildren and just loves Kohanga Reo, and meeting up with the other tamariki.

Some of the kaiawhina belong to different tribes—Ngāti Maniapoto, Te Arawa, Tuwharetoa, Tainui, Ngāti Porou, Ngāpuhi, Ngāti Whātua—hence the name of our kohanga, Ngā Hau e Wha.

At present I am doing a whakapakari training course of three years, in the Māori language, at the end of which I will be credited with a certificate or a diploma for teaching others as well as doing the Kohanga Reo programme.

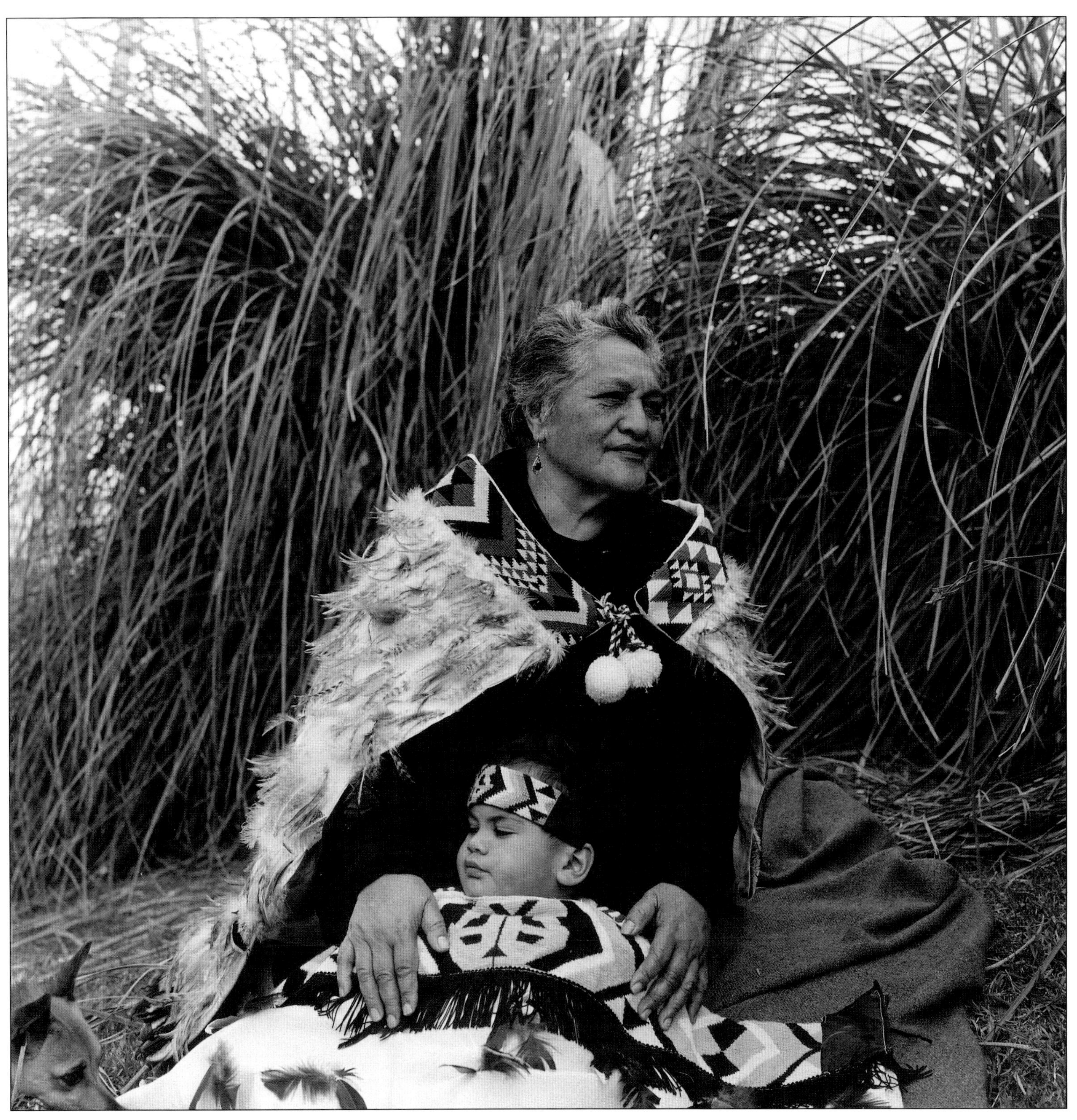

Melanie Simone Kaka

WELLSFORD

Ko Ngāpuhi, ko Te Arawa ngā iwi.

I am a twin, my twin being ten minutes older than me. I am the youngest out of the twelve of us.

At school, Rodney College, I played basketball, netball, volleyball, soccer—I loved all the physical outdoor sports.

I also took up Māori culture and was the leader of the group. My pronunciation was good, but I wasn't brought up to speak it fluently. I learnt a lot of the protocol and the basics on the marae from my parents and on my marae at Omanaia. I'm glad I know them, because we are the younger generation.

I left school at sixteen, and worked at a place called Izards. I have been there since, nearly eight years.

I lived with my parents for twenty-three years. I married when I was twenty-one-and-a-half years old. My husband and I lived with my parents after we were married, for a year and a half.

My husband and I are flatting now with our lovely daughter Trina Faye Kaka. Last, but not least, my twin sister is living nearby and we still keep in touch and love each other dearly.

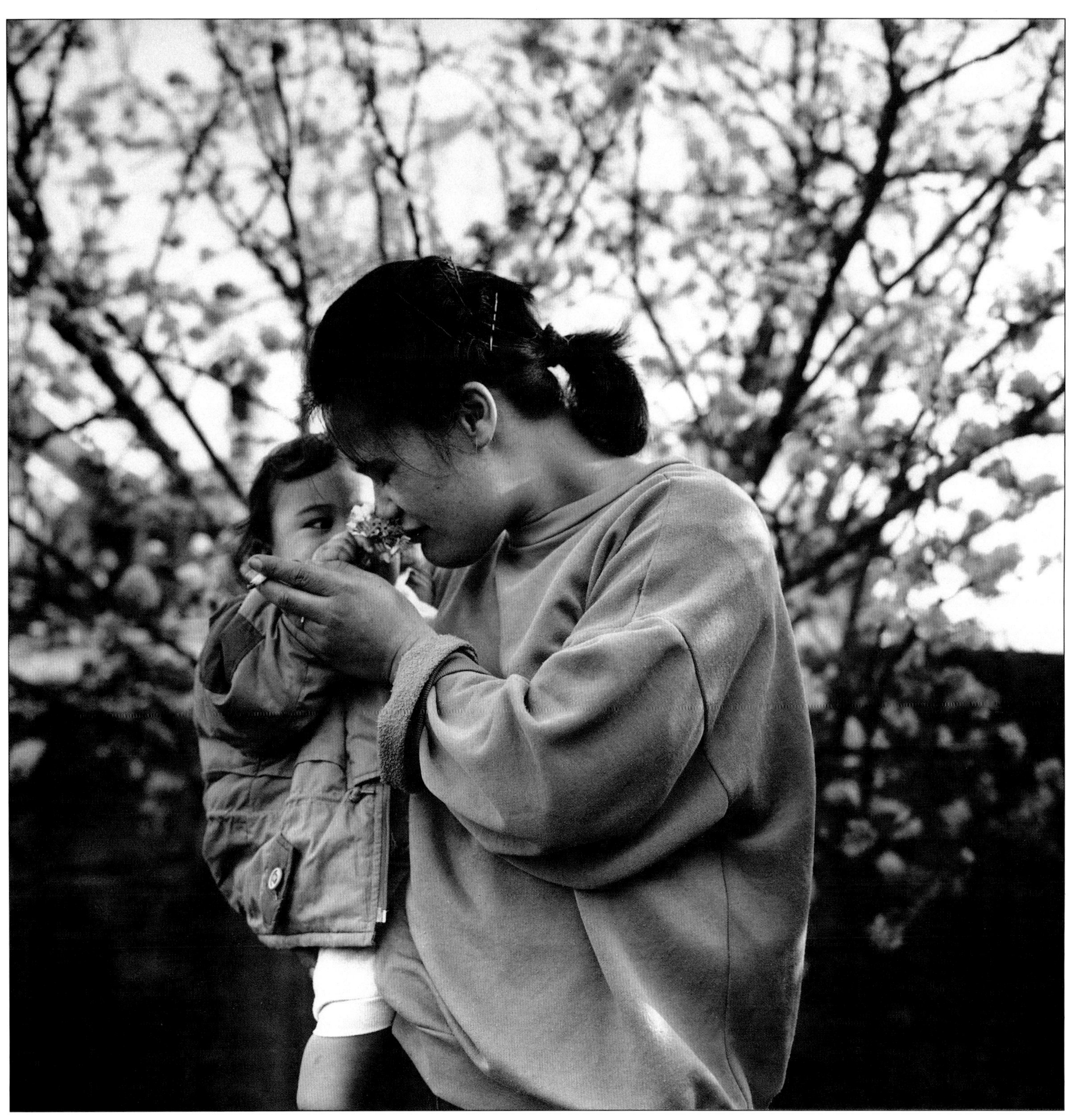

Hema Tata

PĀKIRI

Ko Ngāpuhi te iwi.
Ko Ngāti Toro te hapu.

My grandchildren and their education come first and foremost. As a rule I usually have seven here.

We bought this place in the backblocks for our grandchildren to be able to come here. It gets them away from the city environment. We have nine children of our own.

I grew up in Putaruru, and it was Rauka Bell who taught me to weave when I was about twenty-four.

My lesson was in Māori. Three days after my first lesson she died.

I have her flax growing out there. All my flax are tupuna flax. I weave when I want to weave. I feel free and at peace when I am weaving. A kete can look totally different when my heart is not in it.

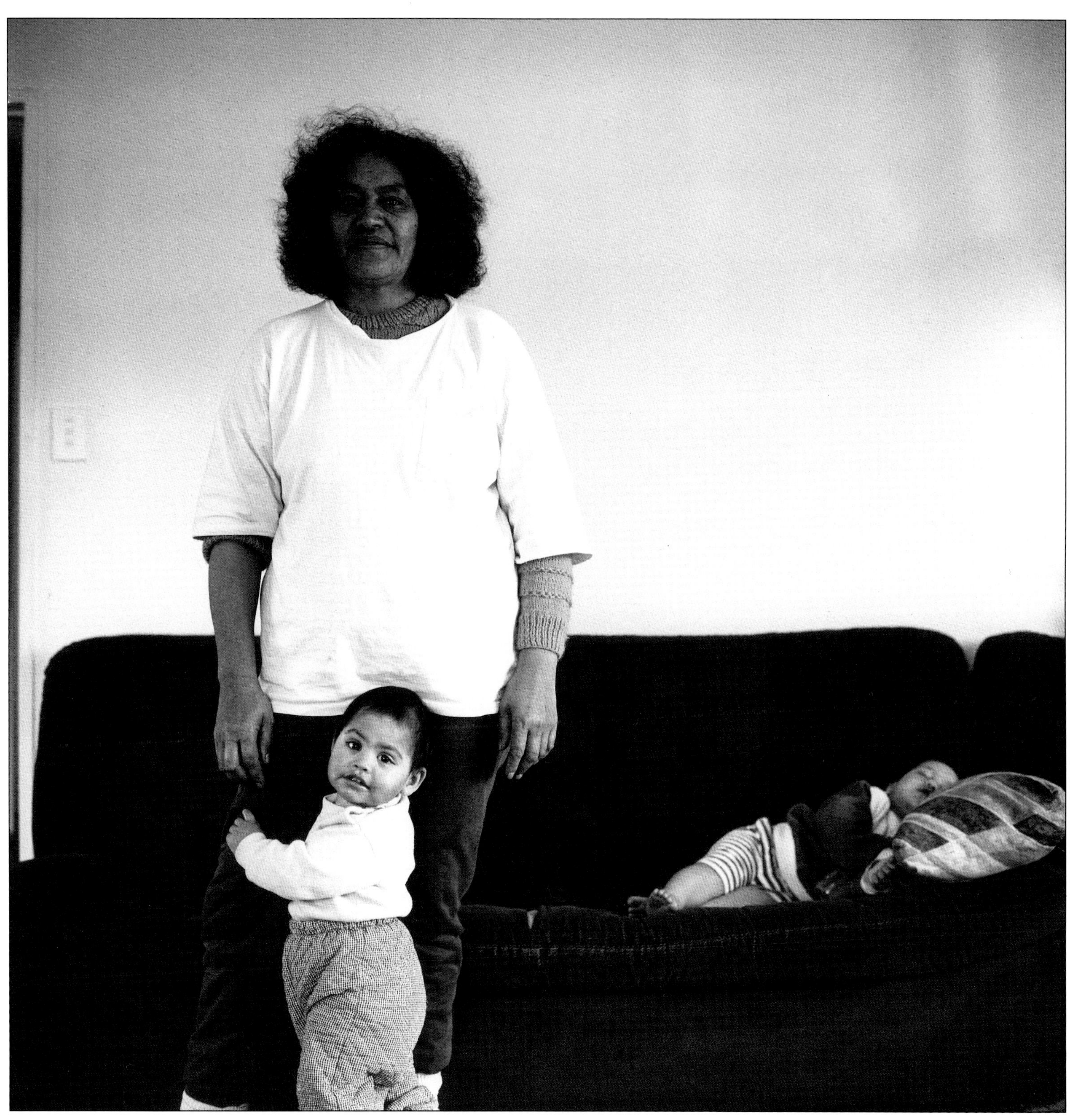

Carol Ashby

PORT ALBERT

Ko Ngāti Whātua te iwi.
Ko Tokatoka te maunga.
Ko Kaipara te moana.
Ko Te Mahuhu-o-te-Rangi te waka.

I was born and brought up in Auckland during the time of trams down Queen Street, and blocks of ice being delivered on shoulders from trucks to homes, and ice cream being kept in canvas bags with dry ice. This was also the time of shilling gas meters.

As a mother and a grandmother I have been through a lot of changes. The issues I find interesting and absorbing are women's issues, of which I am involved in cervical screening, health—diabetes, and abuse—sexual, physical, emotional and spiritual. Whānau and the issues of whānau are a major concern for me.

I do not speak Māori, but can understand the language. The first five of my brothers and sisters speak Māori fluently, but then my parents moved to Auckland and spoke English to help the last four children. I find this really sad and am trying to make up for this through my involvement with Kohanga Reo.

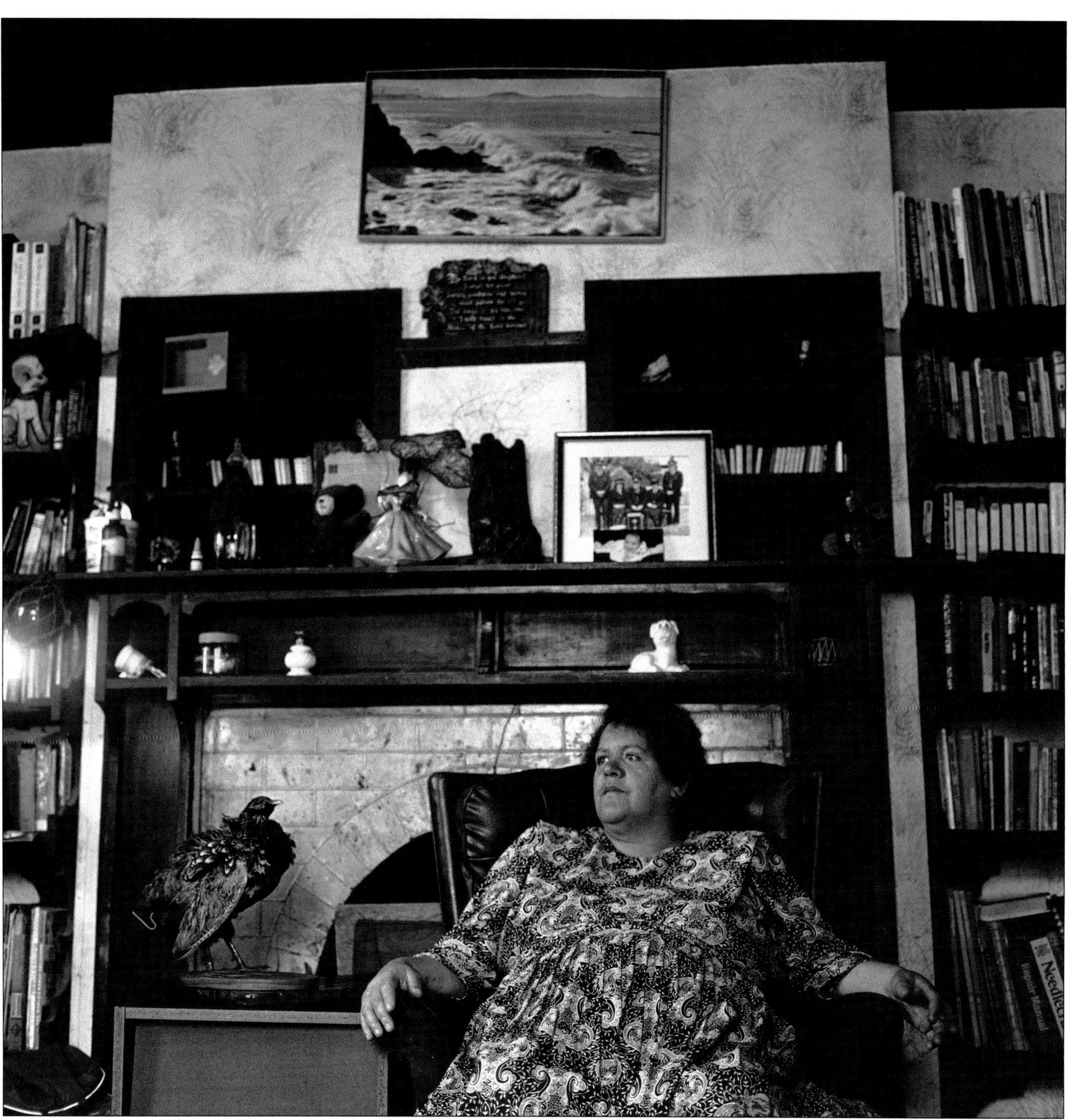

Pare Maraea Korewha

WELLSFORD

Kia ora.
Tēnā koutou, tēnā koutou, tēnā koutou katoa.

Ko Ngāpuhi te iwi.
Ko Ngāti Torohina te hapu.
Ko Mataatua te waka.
Ko Mataka te maunga.
Ko Purerua te awa.
Ko Pa-te-Aroha te marae.

I was born and raised during the fifties and sixties in a Pākehā environment. We were the only Māori family in our street, with maybe one or two other Māori families attending the same schools.

Māoritanga was something my parents participated in if they went back to a family hui. We were left in Auckland with babysitters.

So you can imagine the culture shock I got on meeting my husband's family. I couldn't wait to get back to my parents to tell them about the heaps of Māori people I met, and all from the one family!

We went to live in Wellsford, which was very difficult for me. My husband's whānau and extended whānau and friends would watch me tottering up the street in 'heels' to shop, and before long I earned myself the term of being a stuck-up, 'Pākehā-fied' Māori.

After separating for two years from my husband, coming back was difficult. We were both brought up in totally different worlds. However, after counselling we decided we had hit rock-bottom and we could only, with determination and hard work, go forward.

Through my children I became conscious of being Māori. I have learnt so much about Māori culture, taha Māori, and developed a need to know more—all in the space of about four years.

Suddenly I see my children growing up and leaving home and I need a more stimulating challenge to do something positive.

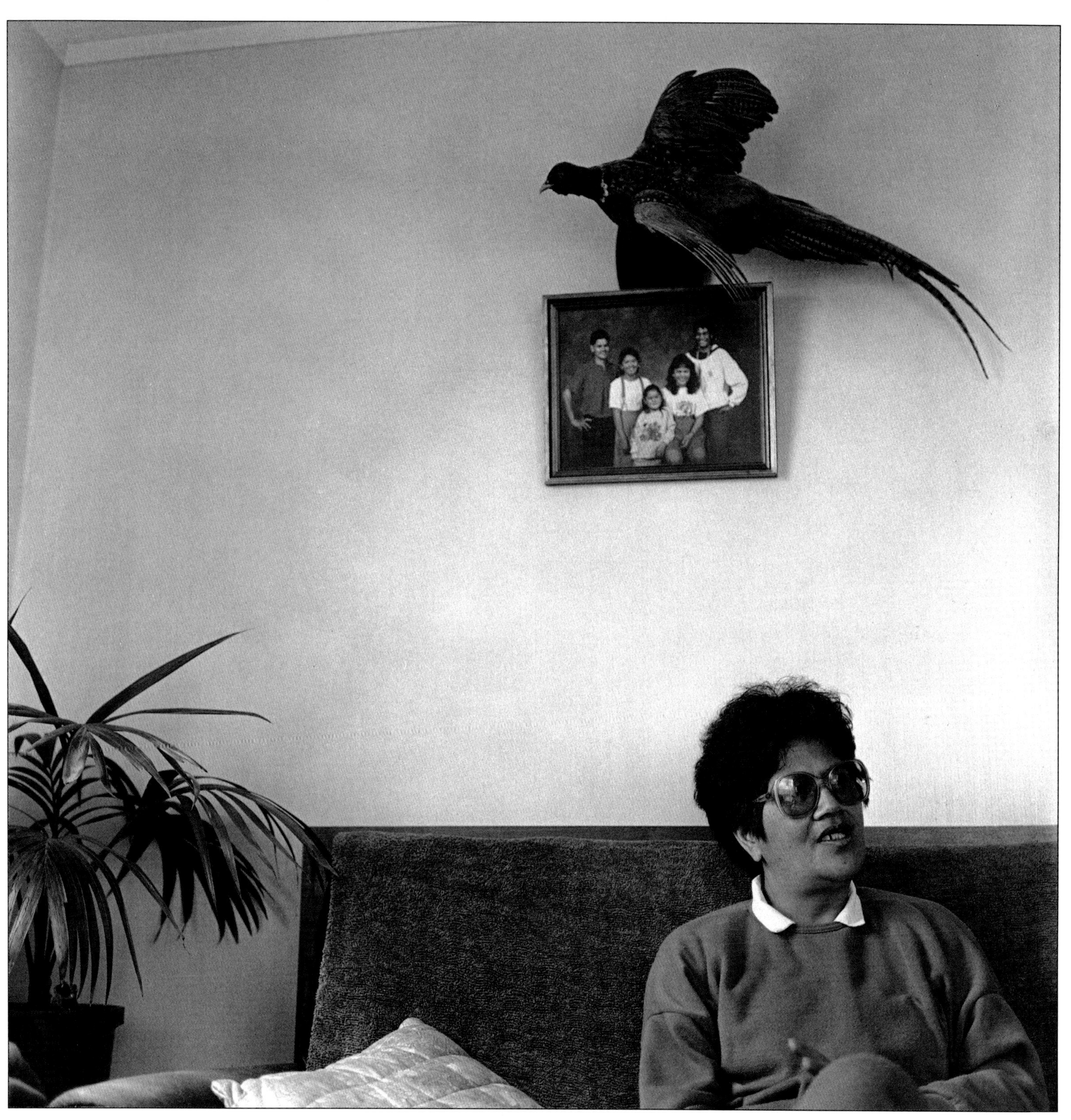

Terauoriwa Tamihana Tunui

ORUAWHARO

Ko Ngāti Whātua te iwi.

I was born in Oruawharo in the year 1934. My Dad's name was Weneti Tamihana, also known as Len Thompson, and my mother was Merehana Pirongia Hemana. I had two older brothers.

When I first started school at the Oruawharo Native School, my Dad was farming on our ancestral land known as Waingohi.

Then my mother died of TB. Not long after she died the house was pulled down. My brothers had left home. This left just my Dad and me.

With no stable place to live, we became drifters, staying with friends and relations.

About 1944 my Dad had a two-bedroom house built for us, and at the beginning of 1948 he sent me to Auckland Girls Grammar School. I can still remember not wanting to go. Not only would I miss my beloved Dad, but I felt so inadequate in coping with the 'big city'.

I was fifteen when I got a call that my Dad was dying. I was very upset, as my Dad was my whole life. Fortunately I was home for two days before he died.

My Dad had paid my schooling for another eighteen months, so to please him I returned to Auckland.

At the end of 1951 I left school. I wanted to go to Training College, but started work with the Post Office. Soon after, I met my husband Rangi Tunui, who is from Poroporo, Whakatane.

Over the next few years we moved from place to place and had seven children.

In 1970 I had my last child, Aroha, back in Auckland. We thought we would probably spend the rest of our days there, but at the beginning of 1990 my husband and I decided to come back to Oruawharo.

After nearly half a century of moving around with my husband and family, I have finally come home to my roots.

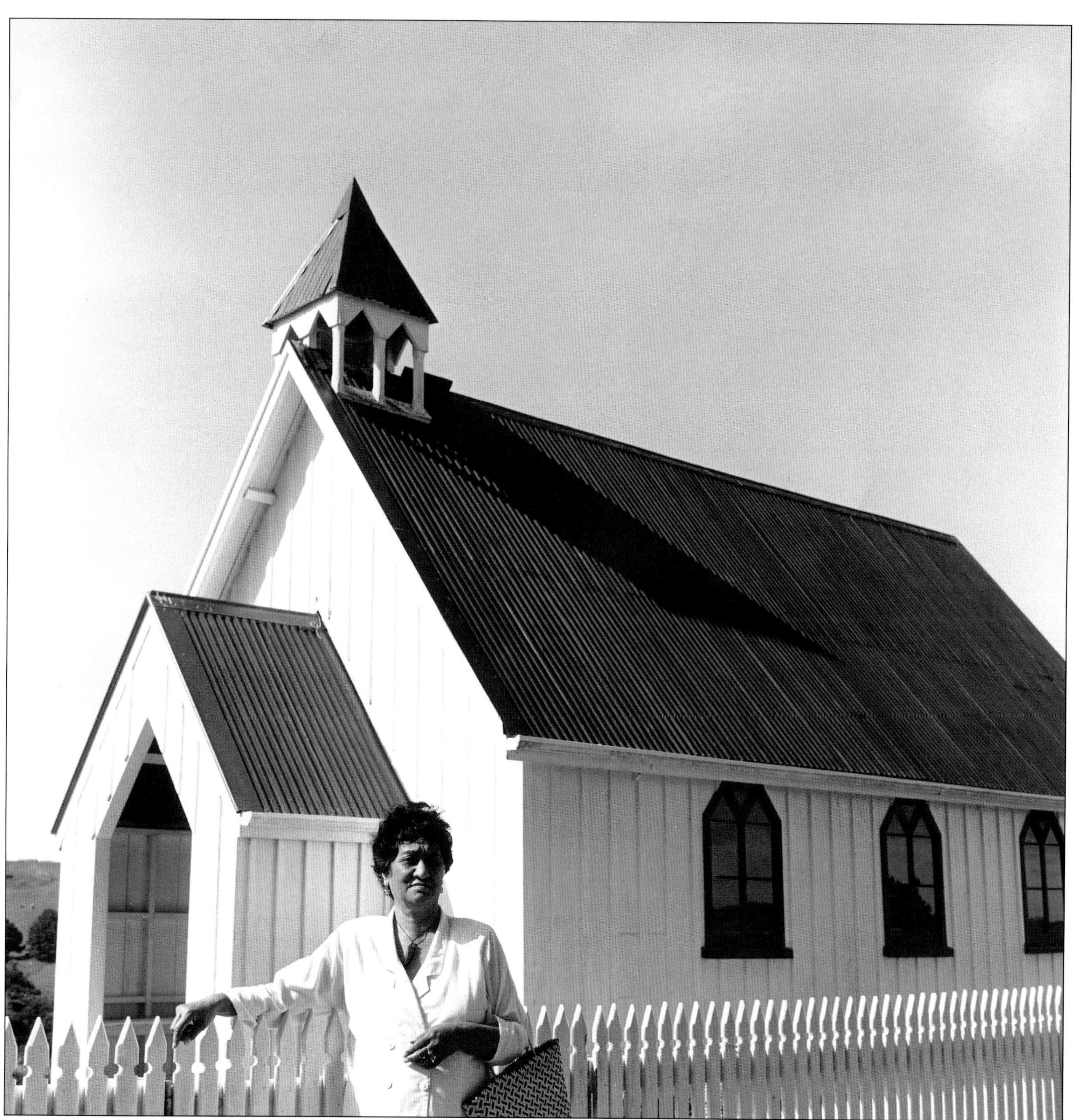

Kitty Wynwood

WELLSFORD

Ko Ramaroa te maunga.
Ko Whirinaki te awa.
Ko Ngāpuhi te iwi.
Ko Te Hikutu te hapu.
Ko Ngātokimatawhaorua te waka.
Ko Werewhutu te kainga.

Tēnā koutou, tēnā koutou, tēnā koutou katoa.

I contribute to our taonga with the greatest of pleasure, to share my experiences as a young girl growing up in Parirau, Matakohe, North Auckland.

I am the eldest of eleven children, eight surviving. I remember lean times and illnesses suffered by many families, our nanny treating the sick with Māori rongoā, an area I sadly missed out on learning.

My primary education began in 1936 at Matakohe School. Primary school was enjoyable, but high school was daunting for me. On interview day for third-formers three Māori girls were at the end of the queue. We all wanted commercial typing as one of the subjects, but the headmaster had other ideas: 'You Māori girls are more suited to home science, cooking and clothing,' said he, 'because you can get jobs in hotels, and accommodation is available.'

My language was a no-no at school, and was not encouraged at home. My father said English was the language to get you by. Father was determined also that nursing was the vocation for me.

In 1953 I failed my first state exam in one subject, and it was here that I became aware of the importance of education. Six months later I passed, and I became a state-registered nurse in 1956.

In our community I learnt my reo through our Kohanga Reo. The reo and culture are now being taught at our primary school and college. I am proud of being one of the tutors at our primary school. Today I will continue to foster our reo and culture to the best of my ability.

Noho ora mai i raro i te maru o Ihoa.

For my late husband, Graeme, son, Peter, and mokopuna, Tanya, Cristina and Peter.

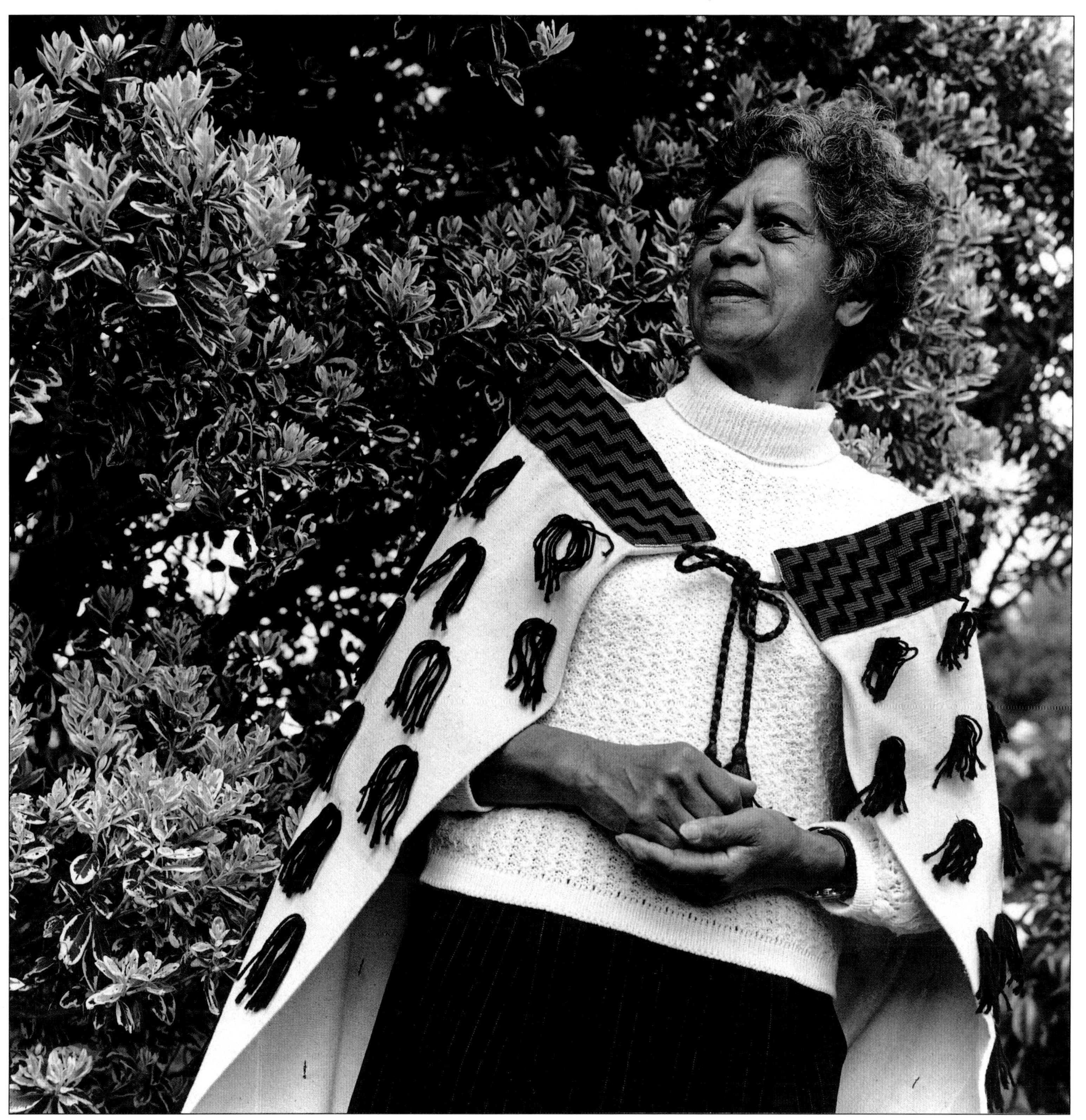

Ngawaina Maata Billington

LEIGH

Ko Whakarongorua te maunga.
Ko Utakura te awa.
Ko Puketawa te marae.
Ko Ngātokimatawhaorua te waka.
Ko Popoto te hapu.
Ko Ngāpuhi whānui te iwi.

I was born to Raiha and Paapu Tohu as Ngawaina Maata.

I remember our house (my Karani Mere's one). It was a one-roomed affair built of stout mānuka and nīkau fronds. The dark shine of the nīkau walls was enhanced by the slate-grey gleam of our mud floor, when not covered by the tamata, woven flax mats, made by my karani. The fireplace, which took up two-thirds of one wall, was the main focal point in our whare.

Many things happened there: the cooking of meals, heating of water for laundry, and bathing during winter. (In summertime these chores were done down at the creek.) Also the drying of fish (mainly eels) was done here, in our nīkau house.

This was where I sat in front of my karani while she brushed and braided my hair as she recounted tales of the deeds of some of my ancestors and reminisced about my pāpā, who died long before I was born. It was a place where our night and morning prayers were said, a place where she had her weekly gathering of old cronies to play card games of five hundred and poker.

Although I was banned from participating, I became an adept card player by the time I was seven years old, through being very quiet and watching.

The fireplace was my greatest source of warmth from the cold of the winter months. The wetness after being out floundering and eeling or just before going to bed—that last grasp of warmth before you dive under the covers!

And now fifty years on these memories are still clear to me. I have a lot to thank my karani for, mainly for making me truly Māori.

He whenua, he wahine, ka ora te tangata!

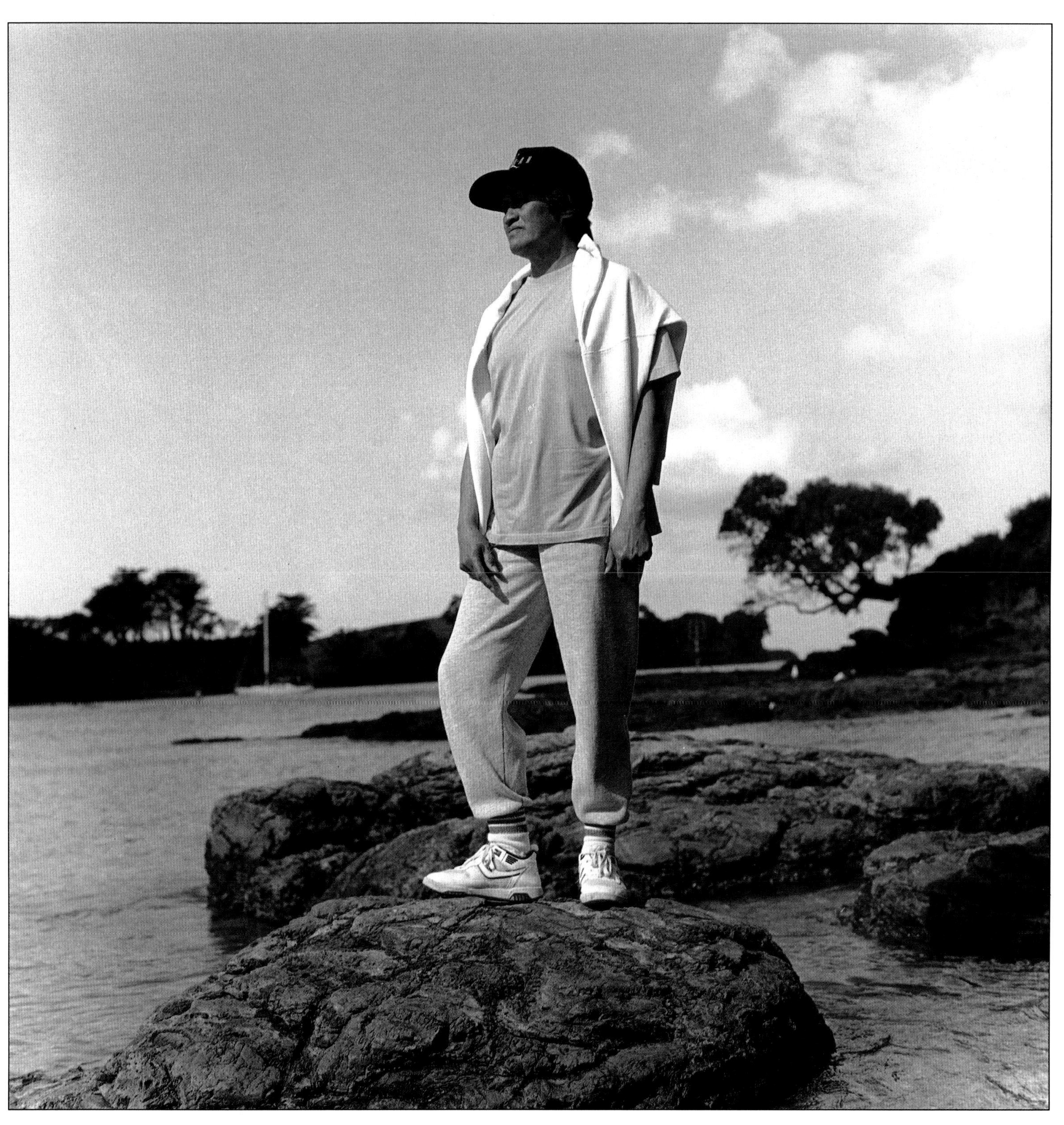

Angela Aitken

LEIGH

Ko Ngāti Wai, ko Ngāti Awa, ko Ngāti Ruanui ngā iwi.

I had a good childhood growing up in the small fishing town of Leigh. My father was a fisherman and we mainly lived on kai moana.

We were treated just like everyone else at primary school, but when I reached college it became a different story.

The college I went to didn't have very many Māori students and only one of the teachers was Māori. So they couldn't relate to us Māori students very well, and we had to try harder than everyone else.

We had a Māori culture group, which was good, but the school would not get behind us much. But no matter how they treated us at school, in our hearts we were very proud to be Māori, and nothing could break that.

Being a young Māori woman is getting better—we are slowly but surely becoming stronger and starting to fight for what we believe in.

I hope that by the time my daughter has grown up our Māori ways will be known by all and be very strong. I hope she also becomes very successful at whatever career she decides to follow. We need more Māori people at the top, instead of struggling to make ends meet.

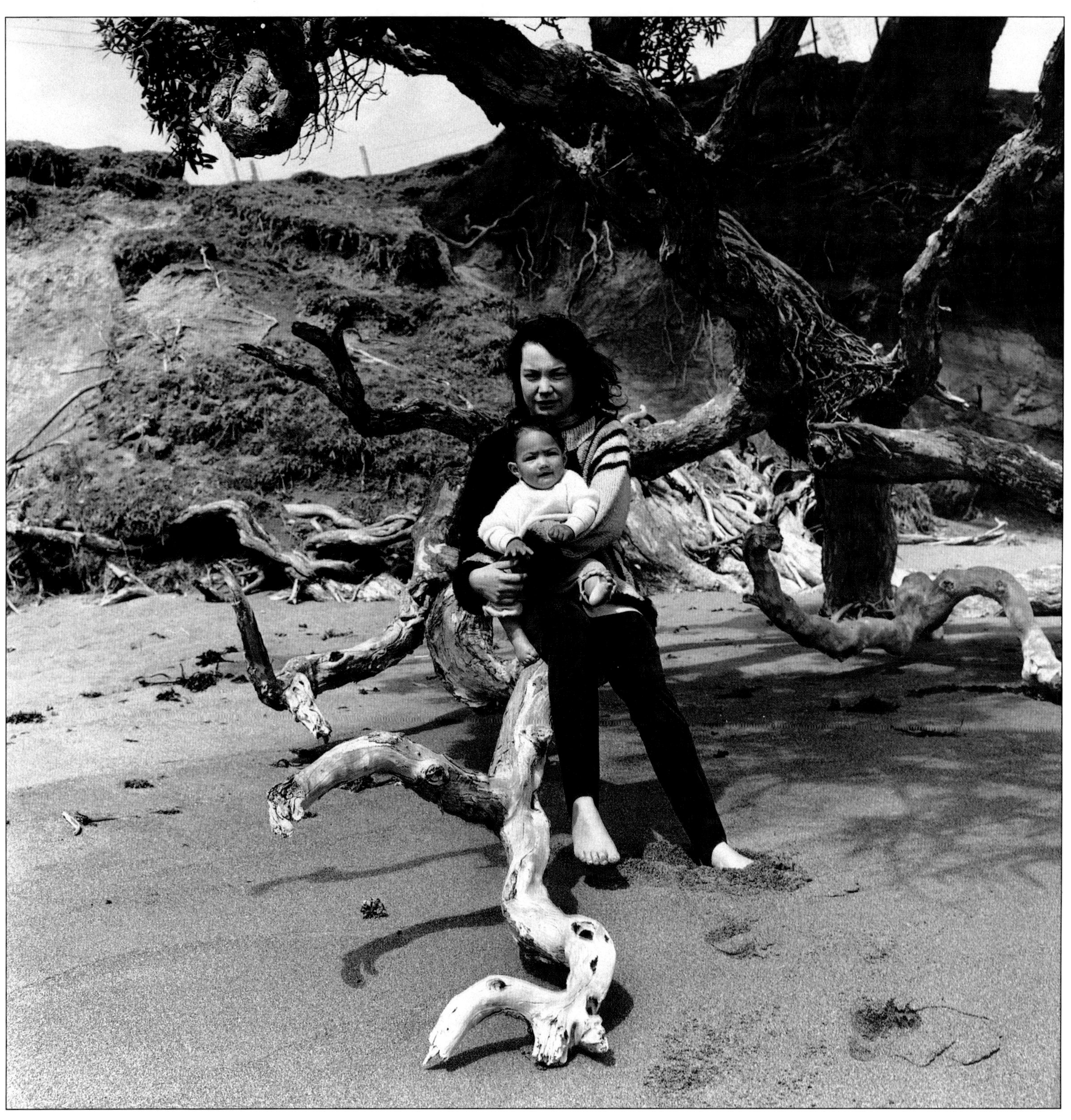

Roxina Brown

WELLSFORD

Ko Pukekaroro te maunga.
Ko Kaipara te moana.
Ko Ngāti Whātua te iwi.
Ko Te Uriohau te hapu.
Ko Oruawharo te marae.

Kua moe tāne ahau. Ko Wiki Brown tōkū hoa rangatira.
E toru a māua tamariki; kotahi tama, e rua ngā kōtiro.
Ko Lucy Aroha te tuatahi, ko Sophia Reo te tuarua, ko Jacob Nazareth Peter te tuatoru, te pōtiki.

Ko ahau te tamāhine a Reg rāua ko Gay Connolly.
Ko Jack Connolly rāua ko Mihi Pene ōku mātua tūpuna.

He kaiawhina ahau o te Kohanga Reo o Te Puawaitanga Me Ngā Hau E Wha.

I was born in Wellsford and have lived there all my life. I grew up in a loving family of six, and I was taught many things about the Māori ways by my Nana Connolly.

I have always looked to the kaumātua and kuia. I learnt a lot at the tangi. These are the times that our kaumātua and kuia can lead and teach us.

When my grandfather died it was very hard. My grandmother helped us all through that time, for we were too young to understand. I loved them so much. I know she would be proud of me and of what I am doing now.

My parents are always there for me too—even at the age I'm at now. My whole family will always be with me.

My children, Lucy, Sophia and Jacob, have all been to Kohanga Reo since birth. My two girls are at school now, and my baby boy is at Kohanga Reo with me. I enjoy the work and feel like a mother to fifteen children.

My husband is a great help. He is learning from me, because he wants to learn just as much as me. We are finding things today are harder for married people with children. We would love to have our own home, so we can live off the land and sea like the elders of the past did.

Māori women today, like myself, are still looking for answers from the past for the future.

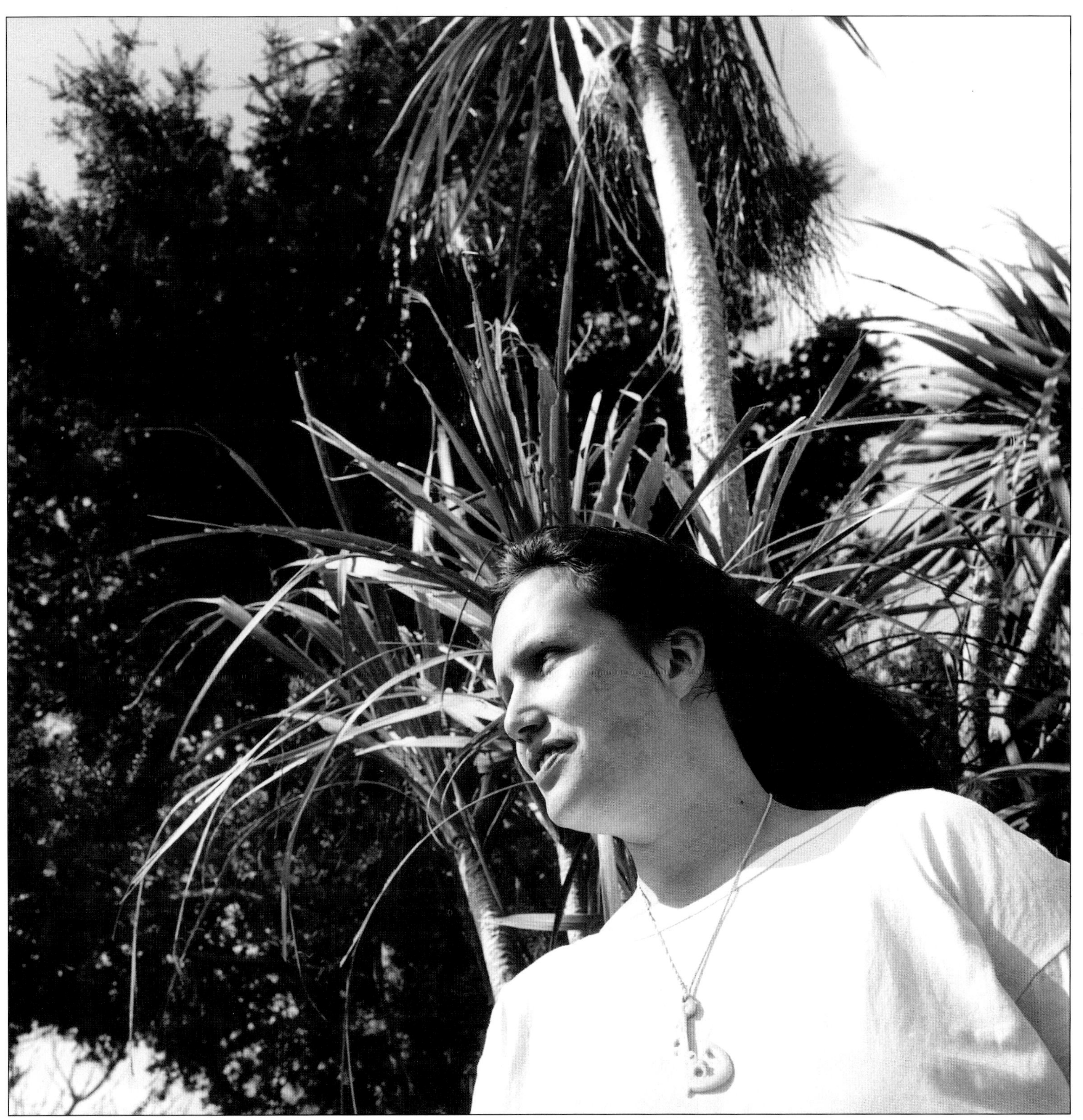

Honey Ashby

ORUAWHARO

Ko Ngāti Whātua te iwi.
Ko Tokatoka te maunga.
Ko Kaipara te moana.
Ko Te Mahuhu-o-te-Rangi te waka.

I never thought of myself as a Māori. I was born and bred in the city, and of course the language was hardly spoken at home. When it was, I never took any particular notice of it anyway.

It wasn't until I grew up that I actually thought of myself as being a very special native of this country. I had grown up among the Chinese, Hindu, Pākehā and Islanders. It was not until I married that I found that my mother-in-law and sisters-in-law always spoke Māori. Well, I had to learn quickly.

Now I can say there is so much I can understand and I am slowly learning to speak it.

I encourage my son to learn, because to know one's heritage is something one can be proud of.

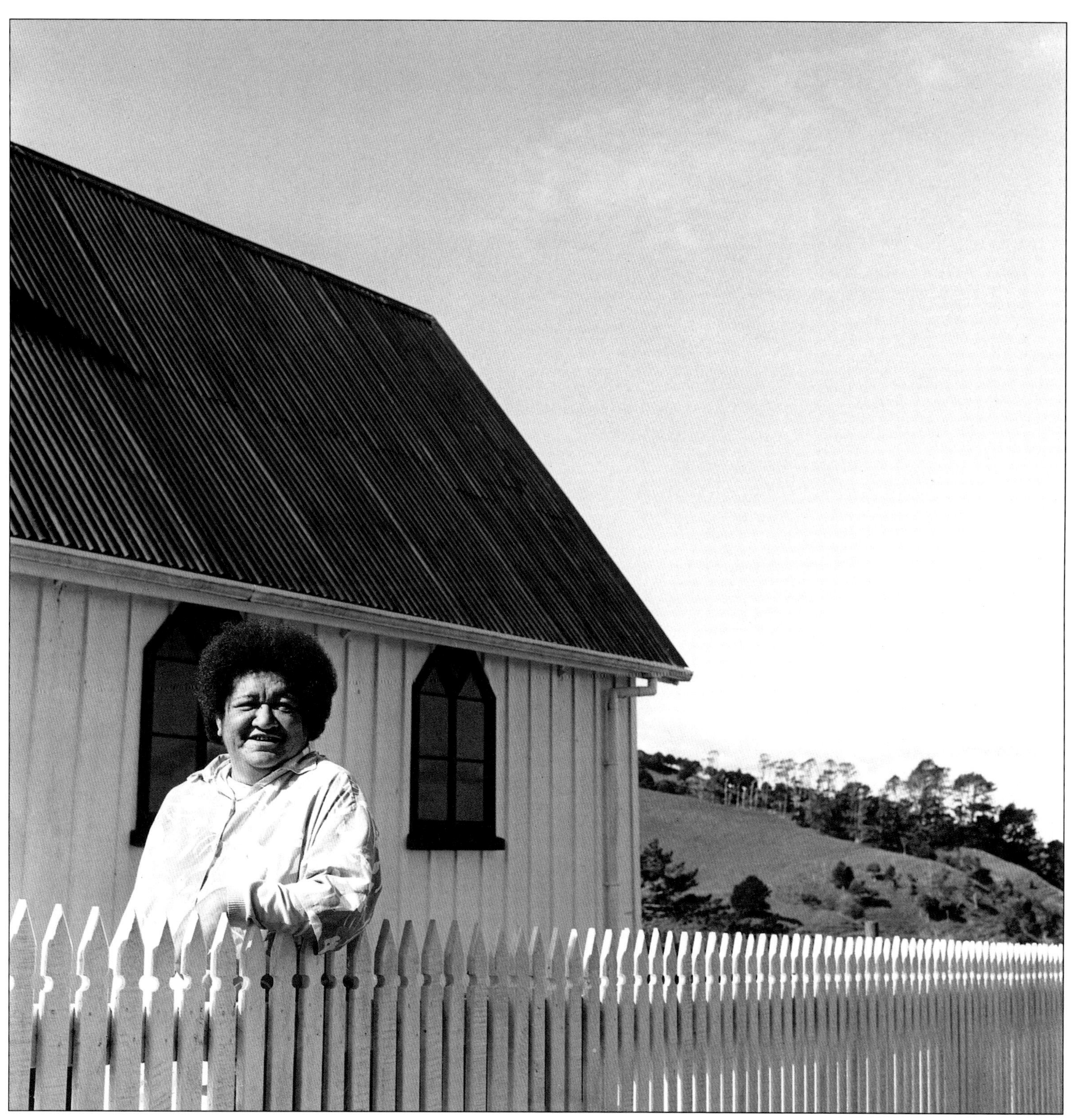

Myra Aitken

LEIGH

Ko Ngāti Wai, ko Ngāti Awa, ko Ngāti Ruanui ngā iwi.

I was born and raised in a place called Pākiri, which is a small farming village on the east coast of Northland.

My great-great-grandfather was Te Kiri. He was a chief and lived at Pākiri, which is the pā he built and named. Te Kiri lived on Hauturu (Little Barrier) as well.

In the 1840s the Government bought Little Barrier against the families' will. They were shifted to Omaha, where Rahui, the daughter of Te Kiri, built a home for her family. One of her sons, Kiri, was my mother's father, and his wife, Tihoi, raised their family on the farm at Pākiri, which is still being run by their grandson Laly Haddon.

We have our family marae at Omaha. It is called Te Kiri Marae.

As children we were brought up amongst our Māori families. We were never taught the Māori language, because our parents weren't taught in their day, as it was against the law. Our lives revolved mainly around the Pākehā way of life. Although that was the way of life for us, our Māori feelings in our hearts were very strong and still are.

Being a Māori woman in those days was hard at times, because everything was mainly Pākehā. The Māori side was proud of being Māori, but the Pākehā side was not proud of being Māori, which caused much conflict. I found I was trying to live two separate lives, and it was difficult.

Today things are much better, as our Māori culture has come alive again. We can be proud of ourselves.

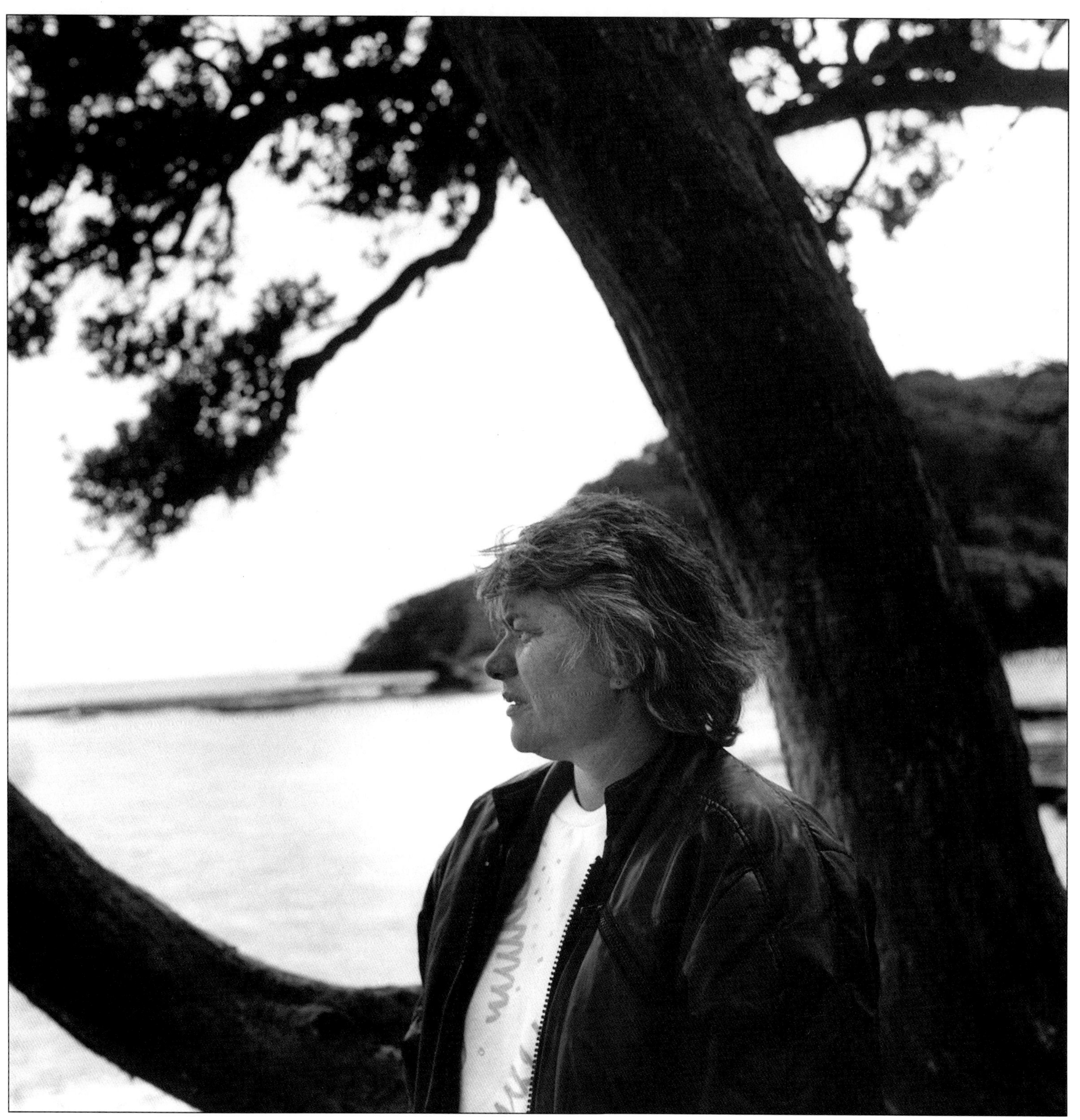

Barbara Huingatini Arena

WELLSFORD

Ko Waikato te iwi.
Ko Ngātiwhawhakia te hapu.
Ko Taupiri te maunga.
Ko Waikato te awa.
Ko Tainui te waka.

I was born and bred in Huntly, a coal-mining town. During my growing years the mines were a thriving industry. My Dad and his brothers worked in the mines and kept food on all our tables. We did not have much, but what we had in our home, we owned.

Then the miners started to strike. It went on for quite a while. There was no money to feed families, so relief funds were issued to the miners' families who were on strike. If any miner worked elsewhere when they were on strike, they were called scabs. It was hard in those days of mining strikes to feed the families.

Yet we had a happy upbringing. Our parents and whānau were always helping one another and their friends who needed help. If you were down and out the whānau were there to help you. Their love and aroha were very important. It kept whānau together.

That is why I believe the whānau of all types must try and teach their children respect and aroha and tell them that the whānau is forever.

That is what my life is about—keeping my husband and our families together. I have a family from a previous marriage, a son I love very much. His name is Wylde Douglas Stark; he and my two grandchildren, Jeremy and Melissa Stark, whom I also love with all my heart, live in Australia.

My husband, Hohepa Arena, and I are bringing up a child named Shakoney Turner, whom we love very much. We have no children of our own, but we have brought up quite a few children that were at risk.

With the help of my husband, the job is much easier. I would never have managed without him. I love and respect him for what he is, a loving and caring person.

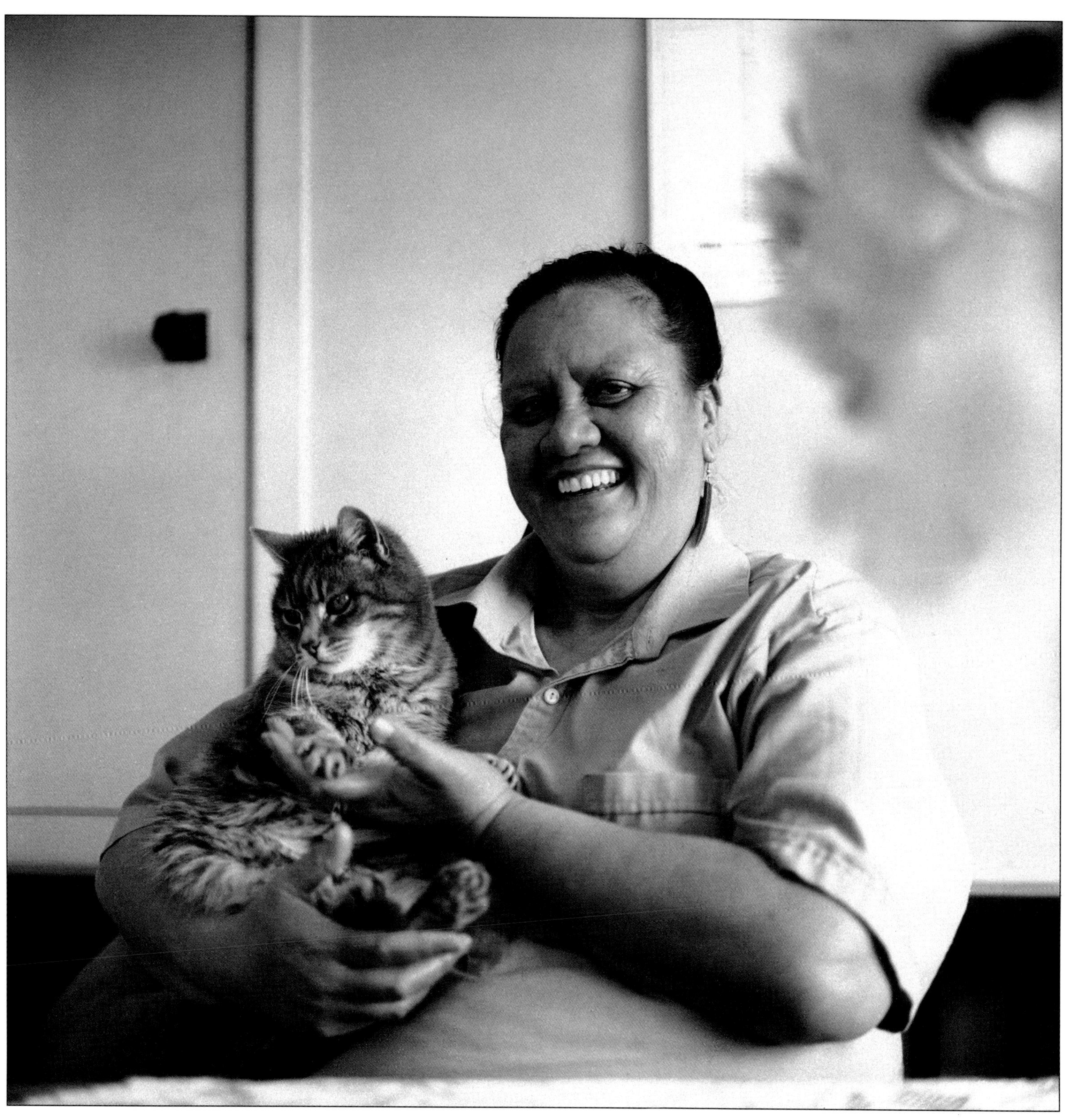

Rozeena Korewha

WELLSFORD

I grew up in Auckland. There are twelve in my own family. I am the youngest.

Most of my young life was spent among street kids, and most of them were Māori kids. I had a home to go to, so I was really just being a companion, hanging out with them, but I got into trouble too.We were the first street kids they showed on television. The 'Eyewitness' crew asked us what we thought we were doing and it made me think.

Then I started working, in a factory, and got a bit wiser.

I moved to Wellsford when I got married. Now I have four and a half children.

I teach two of my children at home. It started when I realised my son was not happy at school—he was very shy and lacking in confidence. I enrolled him in a Christian Education correspondence course and kept him home. He gained so much in a one-to-one situation that we decided to teach our daughter at home too.

We add our own ideas to the programme. My husband speaks Māori and he teaches all of us.

Our children are doing really well now; we know we are doing the best thing for them.

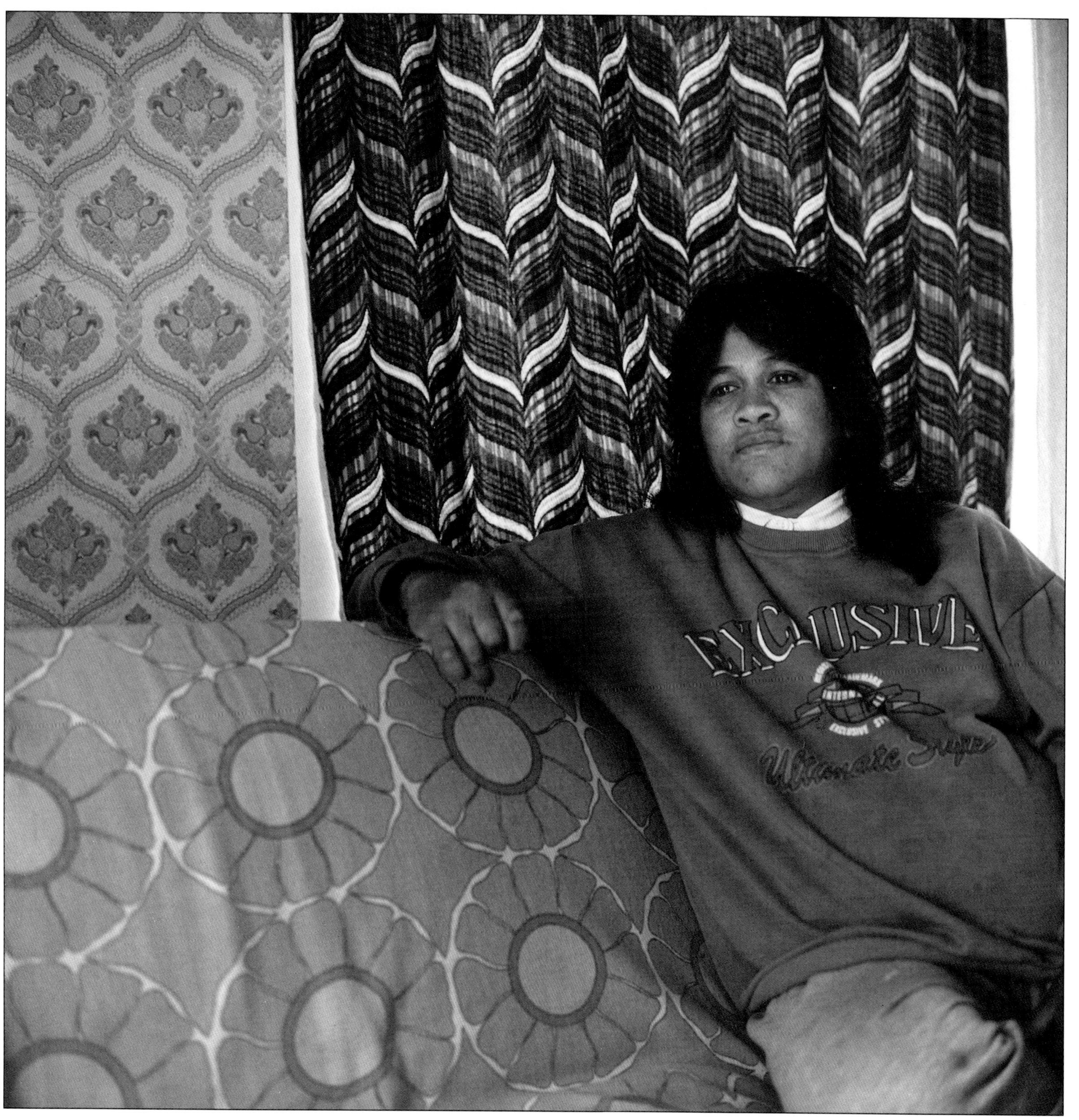
EXCLUSIVE
Ultimate Style

Polly Williams

ORUAWHARO

I belong here. This is where I was born. I am the second eldest.

Our road was by sea. We would go off shopping by boat, across the river. We had big gardens and would leave our wooden house and camp out by the crops and live in a nīkau house. Mother would go out and weed her garden early in the morning. We didn't know what money was. We would take the strawberries to the shop and swap them for hard-boiled lollies.

All my life I was a babysitter, looking after my brothers and sisters so my parents could go to work. I brought eight of them up, even when I got married.

When I married, we moved to Ruawai and milked one hundred and twenty cows. Whether pregnant or not, I milked those cows. We moved later to Waitangi in the Bay of Islands and built a house.

I've had fourteen children. I've got quite a few grandchildren. I've got heaps, many, great-great-grandchildren.

Slowly the children, one by one, moved on and eventually married.

In 1976, I came back here to live.

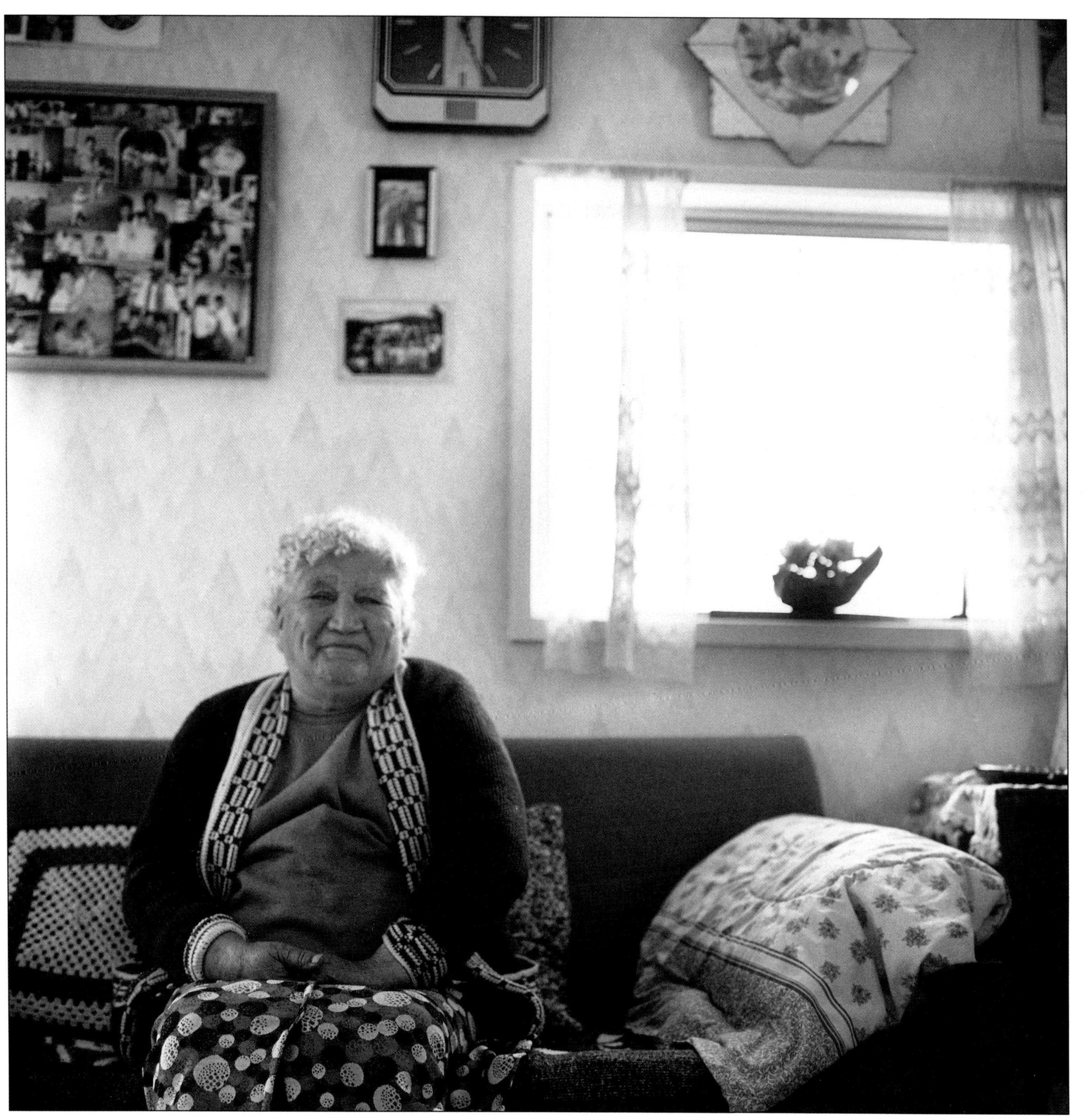

Mary Elizabeth Bodger

AUCKLAND

Ko Te Atiawa te iwi.
Ko Puketapu te hapu.
Ko Manukoriti te hapu.

I was born in 1962 on the wicked west coast of the North Island, at Waitara, Taranaki.

I haven't lived in Waitara for more than ten years, but growing up there has given me a strong sense of appreciating where I come from.

On clear sunny days Mount Taranaki is just beautiful to look at from any angle. When I stand on Parihaka Pā, Mount Taranaki stands solid in the background, surrounded by the green of the native bush. There is a great feeling that my ancestors once stood there with their great chief Te Whiti.

Te Whiti preached pacifism and inspired his people to resist the colonisers without violence, and to demand their rights as people.

My favourite place, though, is the beach, standing looking back at Mount Taranaki, knowing that the presence of the same wairua was felt and respected by my ancestors.

I was the third youngest of ten, eight sisters and two brothers, so times had definitely changed by the time I was born. Māori was only spoken on the marae. When I was on the marae, I was outside playing bull-rush—no time for seriousness; all the time for play.

Socialising at the pā was different for me than for my older brothers and sisters; they had more time to bond with Māoritanga, as their time there was very much a part of their lives. For my generation, social times at the pā were few and far between.

I'm a Kiwi with the pride of being a Māori. My two children are Kiwi of Māori descent, and that will always be.

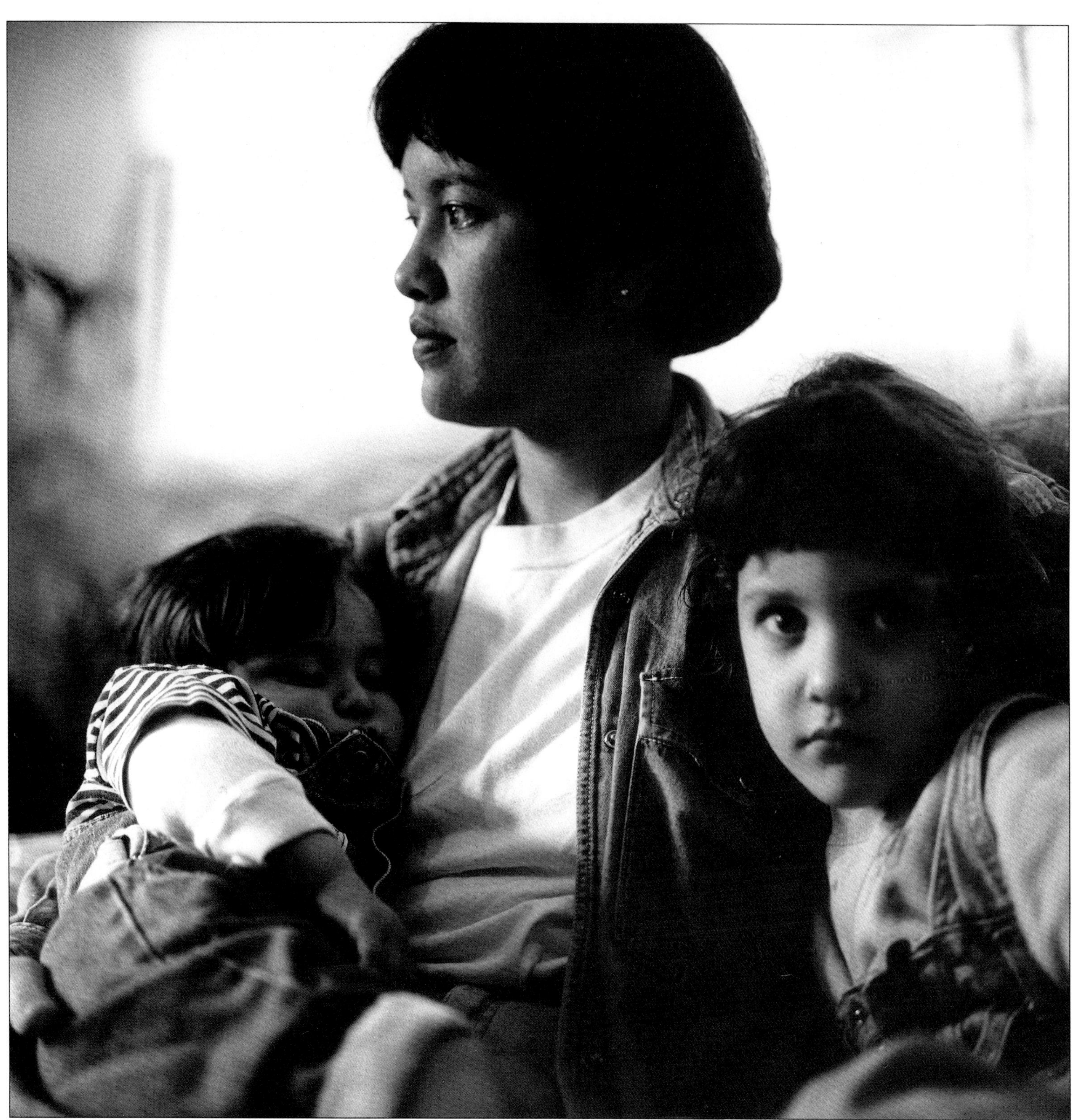

Maudie Katene

MOEREWA

Ko Ngāpuhi te iwi.
Ko Hineamaru te tupuna.

E mihi ana ki a koutou mo tēnei taonga. I haria mai nei ki konei ki ahau. Kua whiwhi tātou, a tātou tamariki mokopuna hoki.

My greetings to you all for bringing this precious taonga to me and all generations to come.

I am an eleventh-generation descendant of Hineamaru. I am eighty-five years old. I grew up on our family farm in Motatau. I was educated at Motatau and Waiomio Māori Schools and Pokapu Public School. I left school and went back farming.

I married and we had eight children, fostering six, and adopting two. I lost my husband in 1978.

I am a past member of the Otiria Marae Women's Committee, and taught Sunday school with Methodist deacons and ministers in the community. I joined the Matarāua Women's Institute in 1948 and the Moerewa Women's Welfare League in 1949, and was a delegate to the first conference in Wellington in 1951 and in Auckland in 1952.

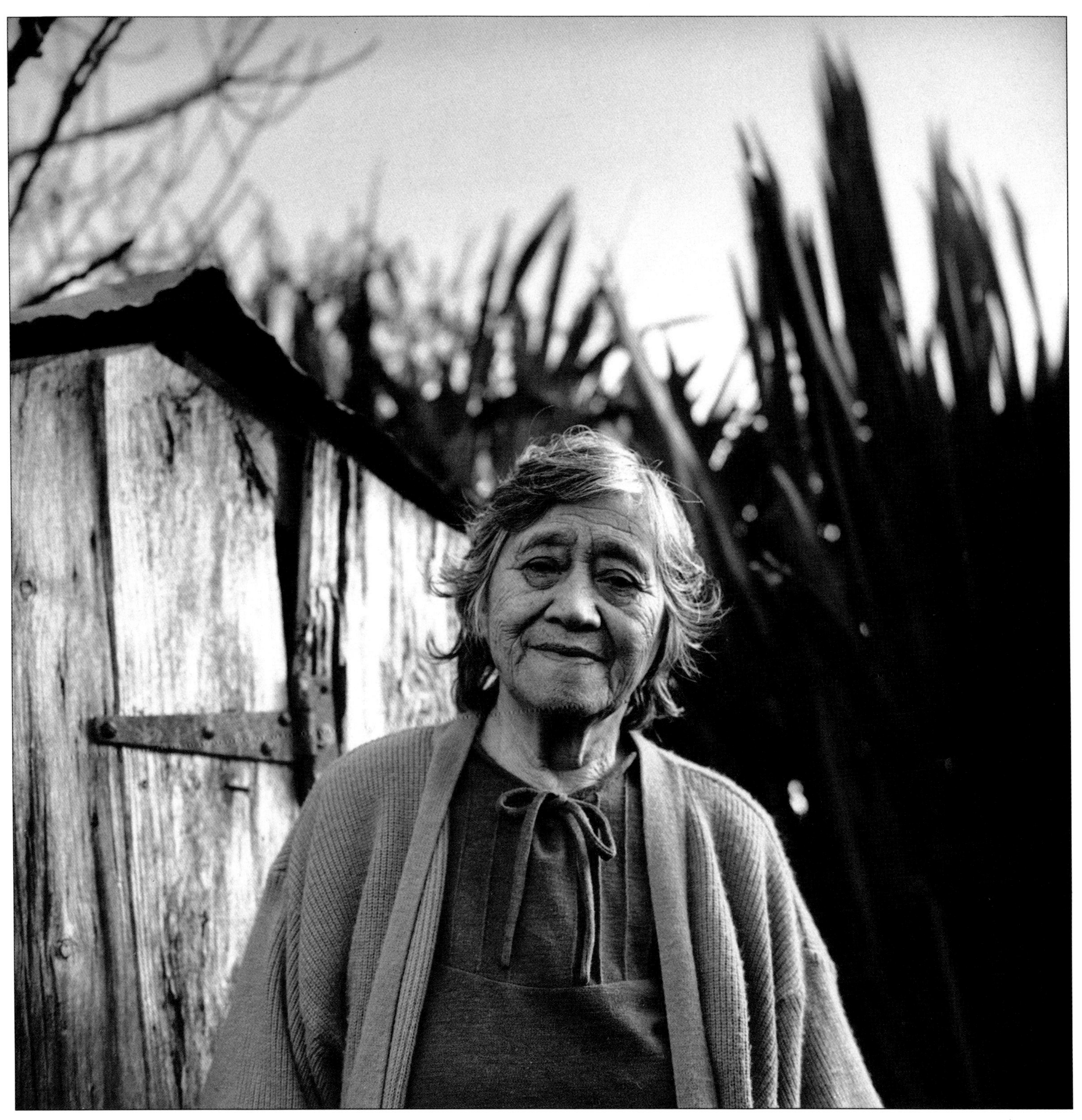

Francis Mary Bray

KAWAKAWA

Ko Ngāti Raumati, ko Ngāti Manu ngā iwi.

I went to Pakaru School. My schooling finished at standard six. There was no secondary school north of Whangarei then. My brother was sent away to school, because he was a boy. His schooling was thought to be more important.

I used to run the Post Office here, and then I went to Auckland. My first job there was working for an Englishwoman for five shillings, being at her beck and call as a housekeeper. Then I worked for a hairdresser and was her housekeeper. When I came home I worked in the drapery department in Kawakawa, till after I got married. I then produced five kids.

I had never been on a marae until I was eighteen. We were brought up as European. I've been to language classes, and understand but cannot speak the language.

Well, I love this valley. I've always lived here. I've been around the world, and I wouldn't live anywhere else.

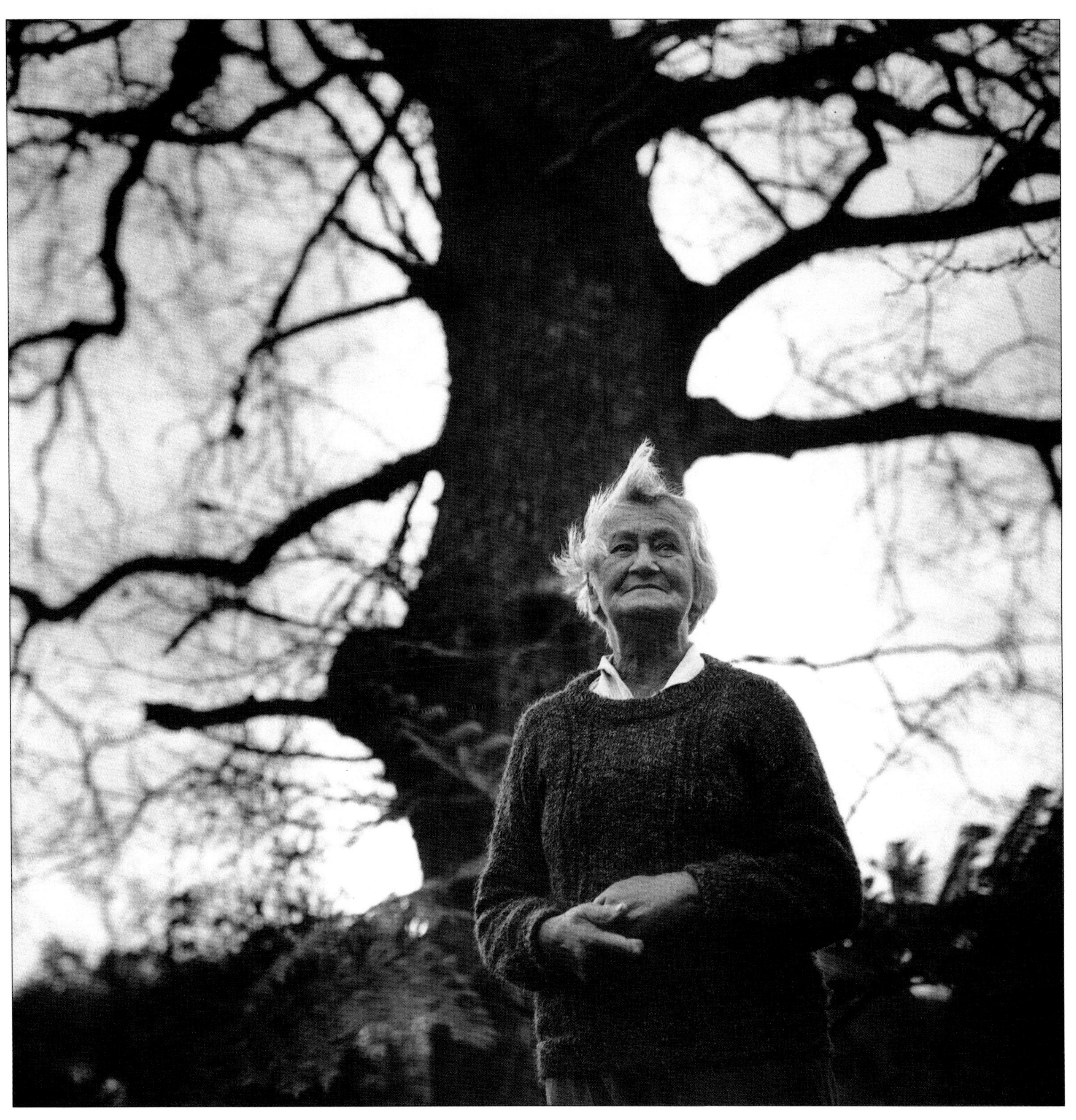

FRANCIS MARY BRAY ▪ 71

Tepara Mabel Waititi

MOTATAU

Ngāti Tetarawa, Te Orewai, Ngāti Hine ngā hapu.
Ngāpuhi ngā iwi.

My father is Pakira Henare Henare, and my mother is Te Riuroa Te Rata Tipene. I was born on 5 February 1916 at Motatau.

I went to the local Native School, gaining a Proficiency Certificate and a scholarship to Queen Victoria School in Auckland in 1931.

When I returned to Motatau, I found the people were beginning to fell and mill timber for the Waitangi Whare Runanga. Every day I would ride on horseback with my mother and grandmother to the bush, to cook and feed the workers. All timber was cut down, pitsawn and dragged to the marae to be seasoned until carvers arrived in 1934.

My relatives and I also took part in cultural activities. The tutors, Henare Te Owai and Te Kurumate Te Owai from Ngāti Porou, were both experts and exponents. At the time Ngāpuhi was preparing for the 1934 Waitangi celebrations, in which all major tribes were represented. I shared the lead roles in poi dances and action songs with our tutor.

The carvings for the whare runanga were carved at Motatau by two groups of carvers. In 1939 I married a carver from the second group, Hori Kerei Waititi of Te Whānau a Apanui from Te Kaha and Whangaparāoa.

During 1935 I had begun to help my father in his bus-operating business. I often drove either the bus or the cream truck. I became the first Ngāti Hine woman to gain a car, heavy traffic and motor omnibus licence.

After the war I worked at the Post Office, where I had many roles, such as interpreter, registrar of births and deaths, exchange operator and confidante to a number of elderly, illiterate customers. At that time I also became the treasurer for fifteen different organisations. As well, I have been foster mother to many, including forty-eight teachers—all single people from throughout the North Island.

When I retired in 1981, I began teaching skills in weaving, and became more active in encouraging our people to use and relearn te reo Maori. On 2 October 1984 I opened a Kohanga Reo in Motatau, and today I am one of the tutors in the nationwide group, Aotearoa Moananui-a-Kiwa Weavers. I am now 78 years of age.

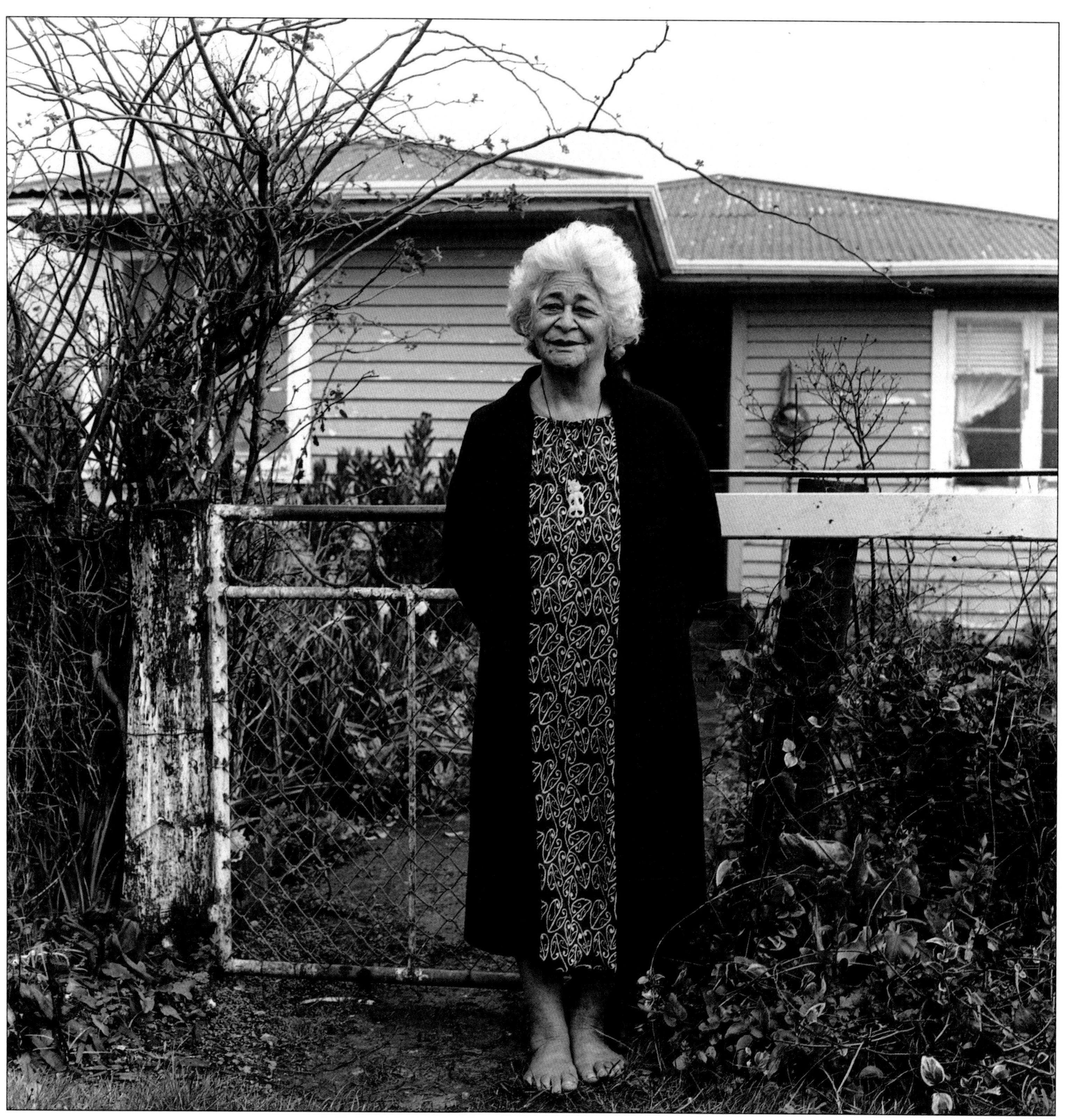

TEPARA MABEL WAITITI ▪ 73

Martha Kawiti

WAIOMIO

Ko Ngāti Hine te iwi.

I am eighty-four years old and married Te Tawai Kawiti. I have had sixteen children, but one died, and have one hundred and forty-six mokopuna and one great-great-mokopuna. I brought up many children.

I have always lived on a farm. I used to milk cows and feed calves with the help of the boys. It was really a hard life for me in those times.

When all the family grew up, we lived here at the caves (Waiomio caves), and my husband bought the property from his father.

My husband died about eleven years ago, but before he died he made a will that everything on the property would be mine until I die. Then the family of fifteen would have our land with equal shares.

Now I live with my mokopuna, Tracey Wells, although she goes home every so often to stay with her family. I am on my own on these occasions.

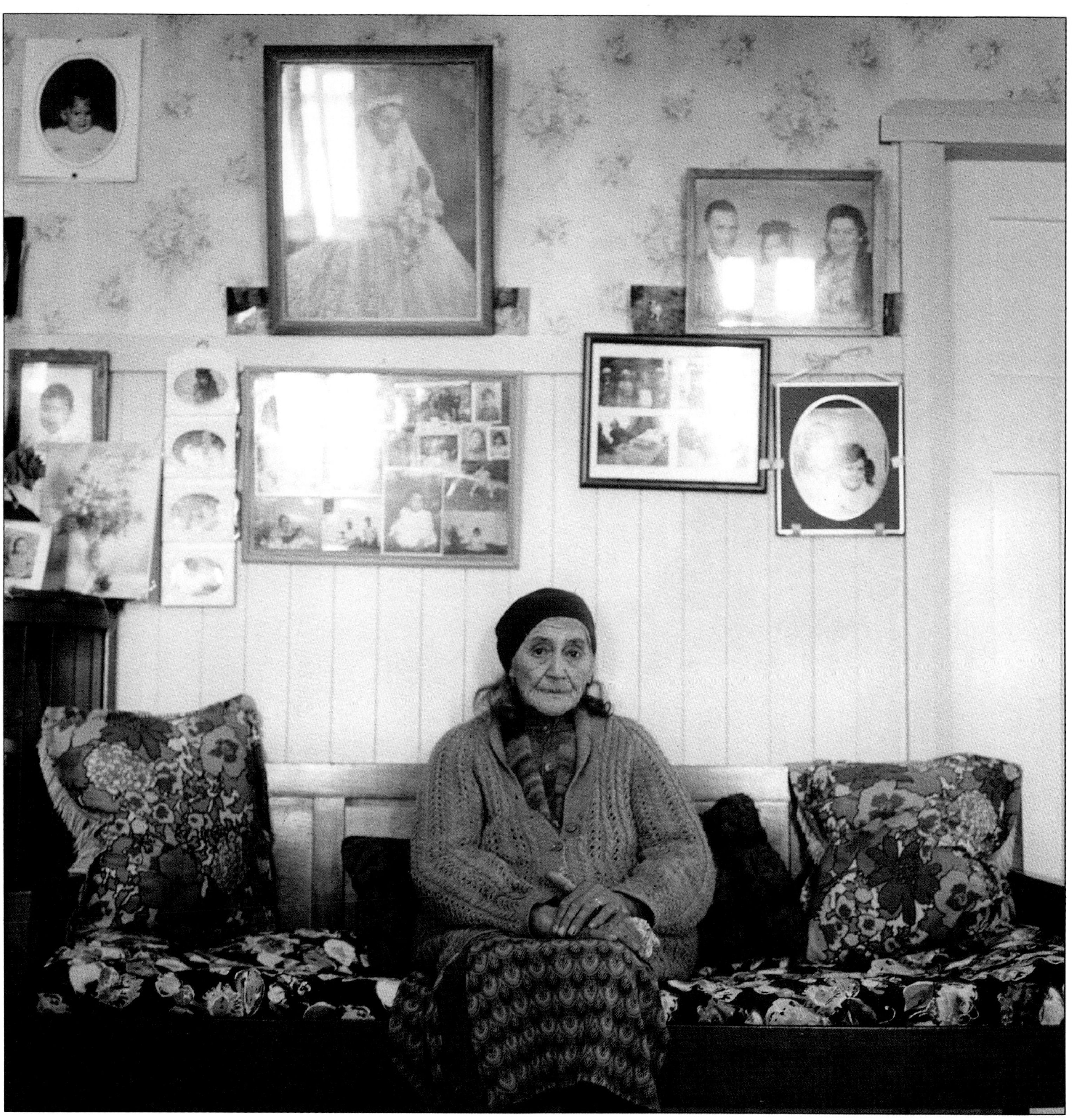

Rubina Hepina Heu Heu Te Rohu Strongman

KAWAKAWA

Ko Ngāti Kahungunu,
Ko Ngāti Porou,
Ko Ngāti Tuwharetoa ngā iwi.
Ko Wi Te Kani Hori te matua.
Ko Merehine Kete rāua ko Tangatakē Kupa ngā whaea.

I was born in Pakipaki, and lived under our sacred hill Parahaki. I was educated and involved in all facets of Māoritanga, and was truly blessed to be chosen by our Paramount Chief Waimarama Puhara to be taught the taiaha.

I have bridged the gap easily between the two worlds, because of my father being a gifted musician and my mother a strict tutor of poi and mahi-ā-ringa (midgets, juniors and seniors). We were wholly immersed in marae concerts, sports and everything taking place in our pā and further afield.

To all our rangatahi and mokopuna, I say respect your elders, learn by their example on your marae. Absorb all you can of our traditions, language, customs and protocol, and you'll be truly blessed and have that extra strength and mana to do and accomplish anything.

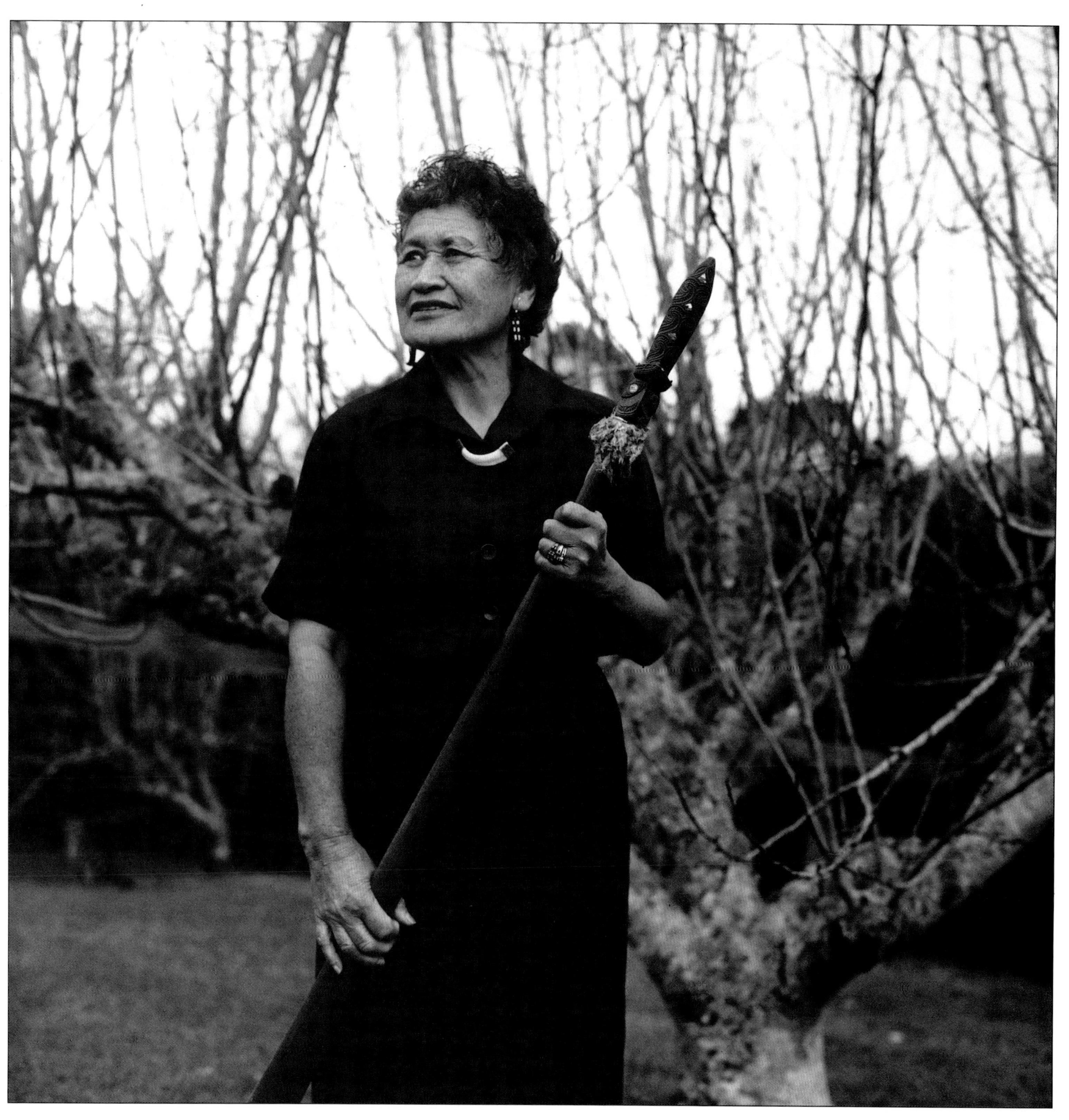

Riu Roa Te Tai

KAWAKAWA

Ko Ngāti Hine, ko Ngāti Manu ngā iwi.
Ko Ngāti Tetarawa te hapu.

I grew up with my grandparents, who taught me mat and kete making. The tāniko work I learnt at school. It was my grandparents who taught me the customs and protocol on the marae.

I am a nurses' home supervisor at Kawakawa Hospital and am very interested in Māori health.

However, I am longing to finish work and start on my culture work of korowai and kete making. This is where my heart is. I want to leave something of what I know behind to the next generation.

If we share our knowledge with others, it will carry on and be shared with the next generation and the next.

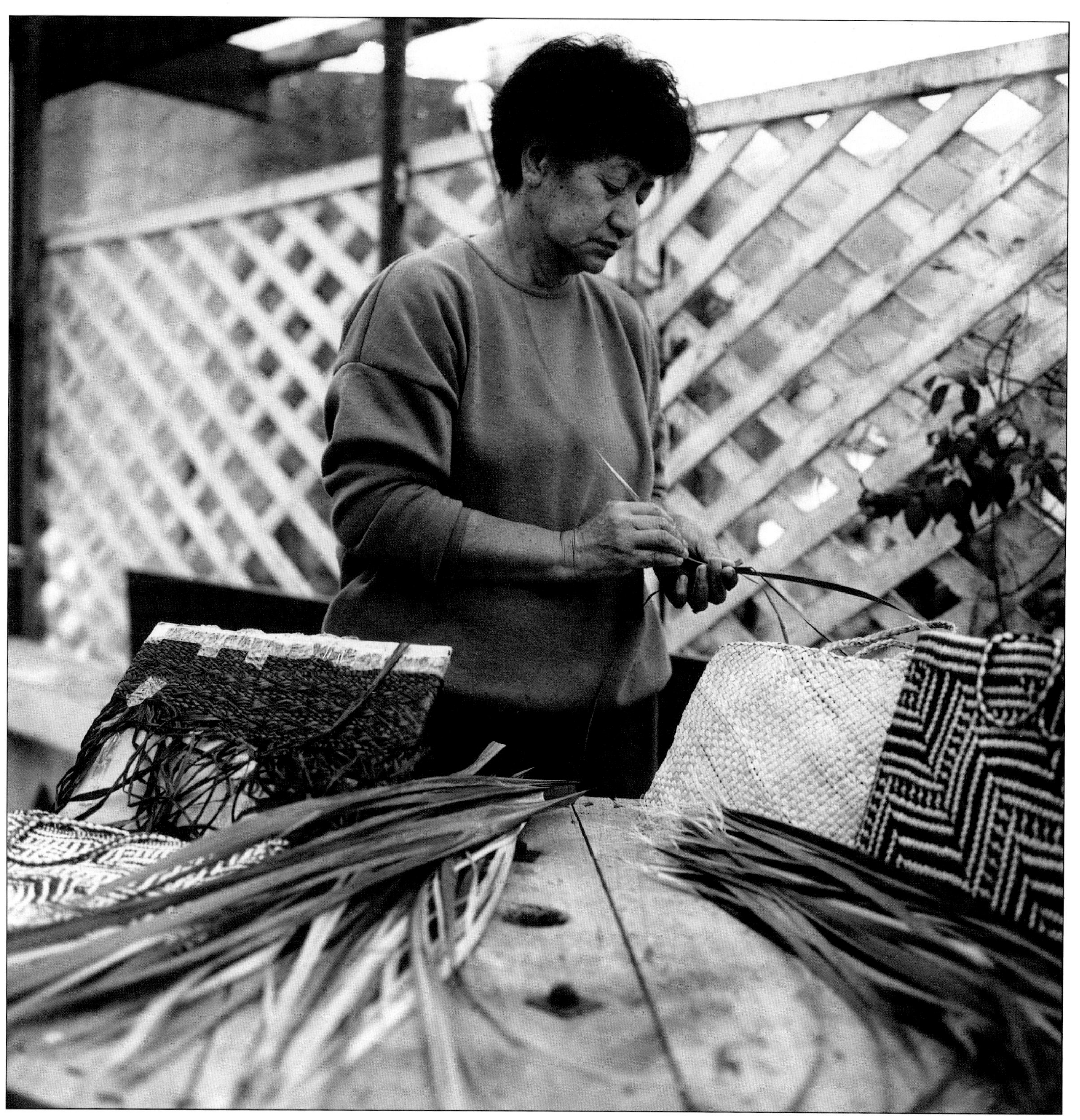

Waina Ross

(14 August 1927–10 August 1993)

MOTATAU

Ko Ngāti Hine te iwi.
Ko Ngāti Tetarawa te hapu.

I was born in this house. This is our family farm; we were born and bred up here.

When I was young, my Mum didn't see the need for girls to be educated, and I had to stay at home and look after the farm.

My first job here was at the Post Office at the railway station. There were plenty of jobs going, and I preferred nursing to working in the Post Office. So I went to work in Hokianga Hospital in Rawene.

I was transferred to Kingseat Psychiatric Hospital in Auckland. That's when I met Ben, my husband. He was a male attendant and an Englishman from Yorkshire. Ben went to work on the Power Board and got promoted to Waiuku. We raised all our family there.

When I first came back to Motatau I had lost my Māori speech, and it was working with Kohanga Reo for seventeen months that brought it back.

I went back to school and did my School Certificate in just Māori subjects, and was fifty-seven when I did my University Entrance.

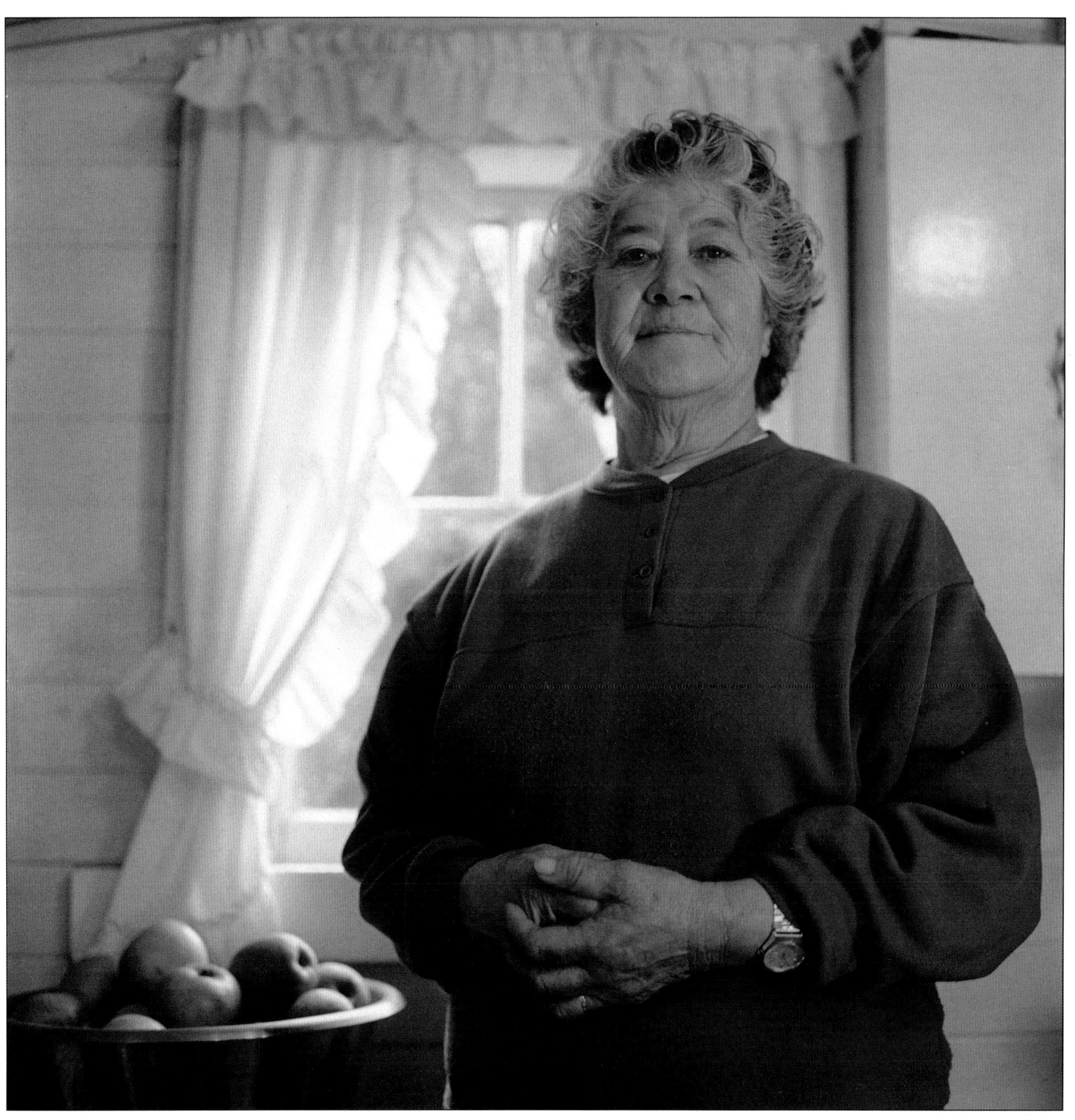

Mary Marara Toi

OTIRIA

Ko Ngāpuhi, ko Ngāti Whātua, ko Ngāti Hine ngā iwi.

I'm Mary Marara Toi of the Panapa and Cummins hapu. I married Paki Toi, an ex-serviceman of the Second World War. We raised a family of three, in the then thriving community of Moerewa. We planned and built our own home in four years, and we became very involved in the activities and youth in our area.

My husband was a very ardent worker for the local Māori committee, the RSA, and the Kawakawa fire brigade, and with Father Merton was the co-founder for our youth committee.

Two other organisations were born—the Waipuna Māori Women's Welfare League and the Roopu Awhina. These organisations helped women in our community to understand the importance of health in the home and education of their children. Through the Māori Women's Welfare League grew the beginnings of a playcentre, which still exists today.

Moerewa is now without many of the big organisations that provided work for people in our community and for many in the north. The dairy factory, New Zealand Railways, and the piggeries closed, and AFFCO freezing works has wound down a big part of what was once a huge operation. Many people lost jobs, and some left the area to look for other work.

Other people still feel the stresses and struggles of feeding, clothing and housing their families in a community that now has little in the way of employment opportunities.

And then there are those in the community, like my own family, who are fortunate. We saw the benefits of that earlier thriving community. We took advantage of the availability of the work, the ideas we heard, and the people we met. And now when I look back at what our community once was, compared to where it is today, I am filled with pride for our children and the achievements they have made.

Me pupuri i te reo me ngā tikanga o ngā tūpuna.

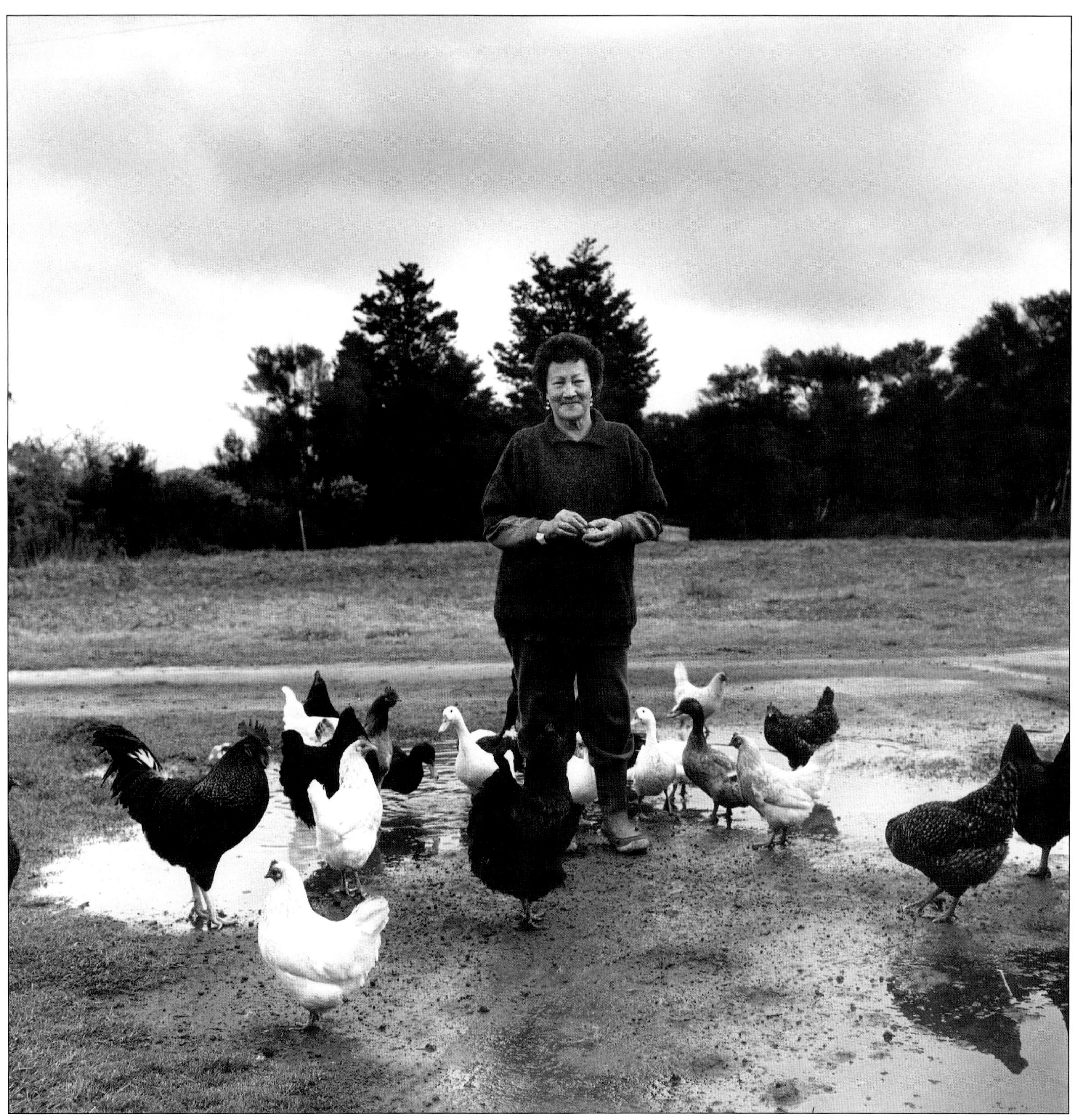

Harriet Simeon

NGAPIPITO

I was born and raised in Kawiti. My father's tribe was Ngāti Te Ara and my mother's side was Ngāti Kopaki. My overall tribe is Ngāti Hine.

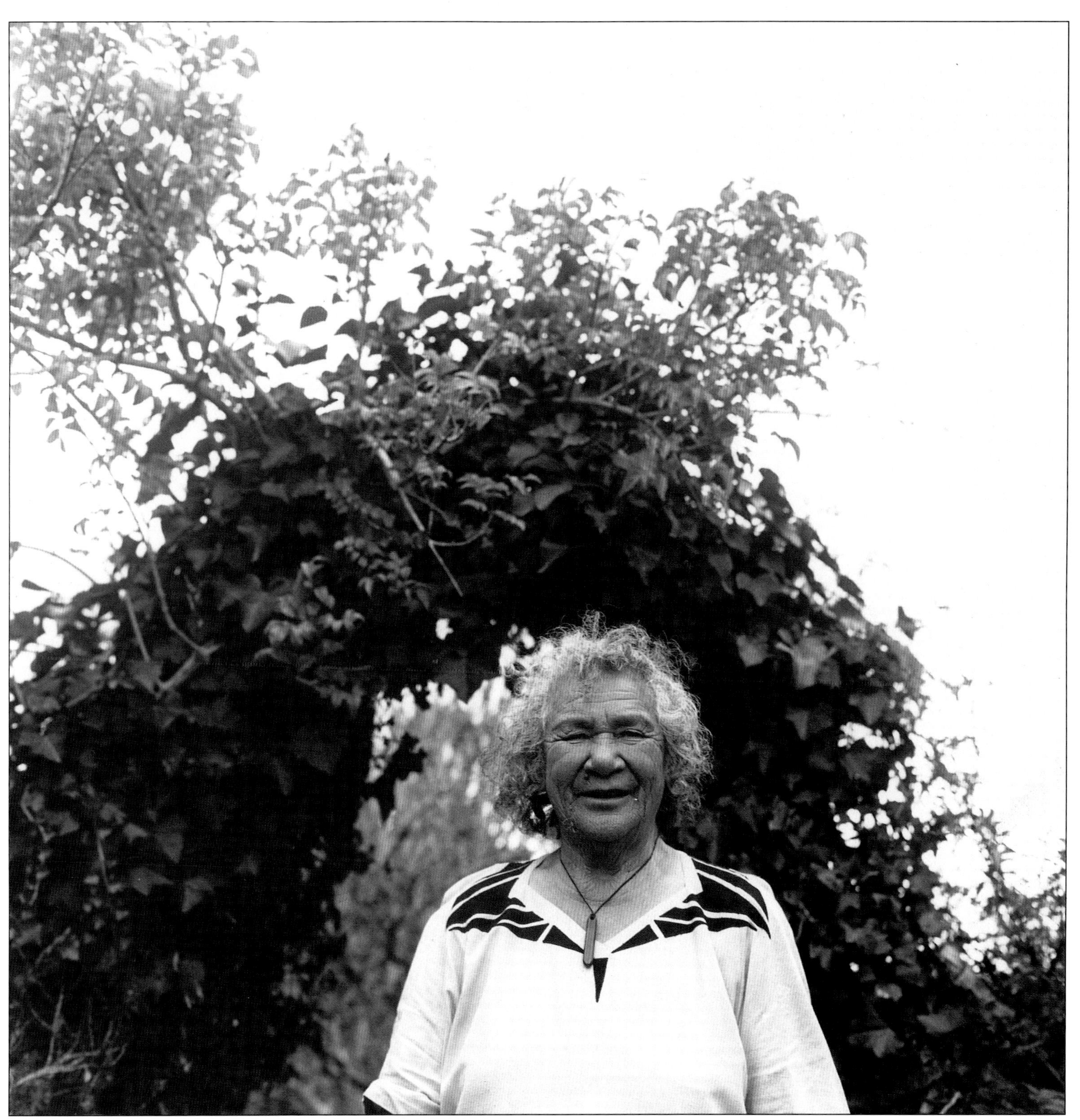

Raiha O'Neal-Karaka Tohu

OKAIHAU

Ko Whakarongorua te maunga.
Ko Utakura te awa.
Ko Puketawa te marae.
Ko Ngātokimatawhaorua te waka.
Ko Honihoni te hapu.
Ko Ngāpuhi whānui te iwi.

Tui, tui, tui, tuia.

My name is Raiha O'Neal-Karaka Tohu. I am eighty-two years old. My hoa-tāne left me back here on earth ten years ago. As my life has always centred around family, I still miss him. His warmth, companionship and great understanding of all things relevant to life, family and culture have been the foundation of our family.

I remember the hardships of yesterday—trudging miles barefoot over hills, through bush, to the local Native School, sometimes swimming across the river with our school clothing bundled on top of our heads, because the one and only bridge had been washed out! Tending the gardens (mainly food), pig hunting (no sex discrimination!), gathering kaimoana. Fishing, eeling, and always watching over the younger members of the family.

From my ten children, I have twenty grandchildren and thirty great-grandchildren, and who knows, maybe more to come! Therefore it is important to me that our children do not forget family.

Kia ora koutou katoa.

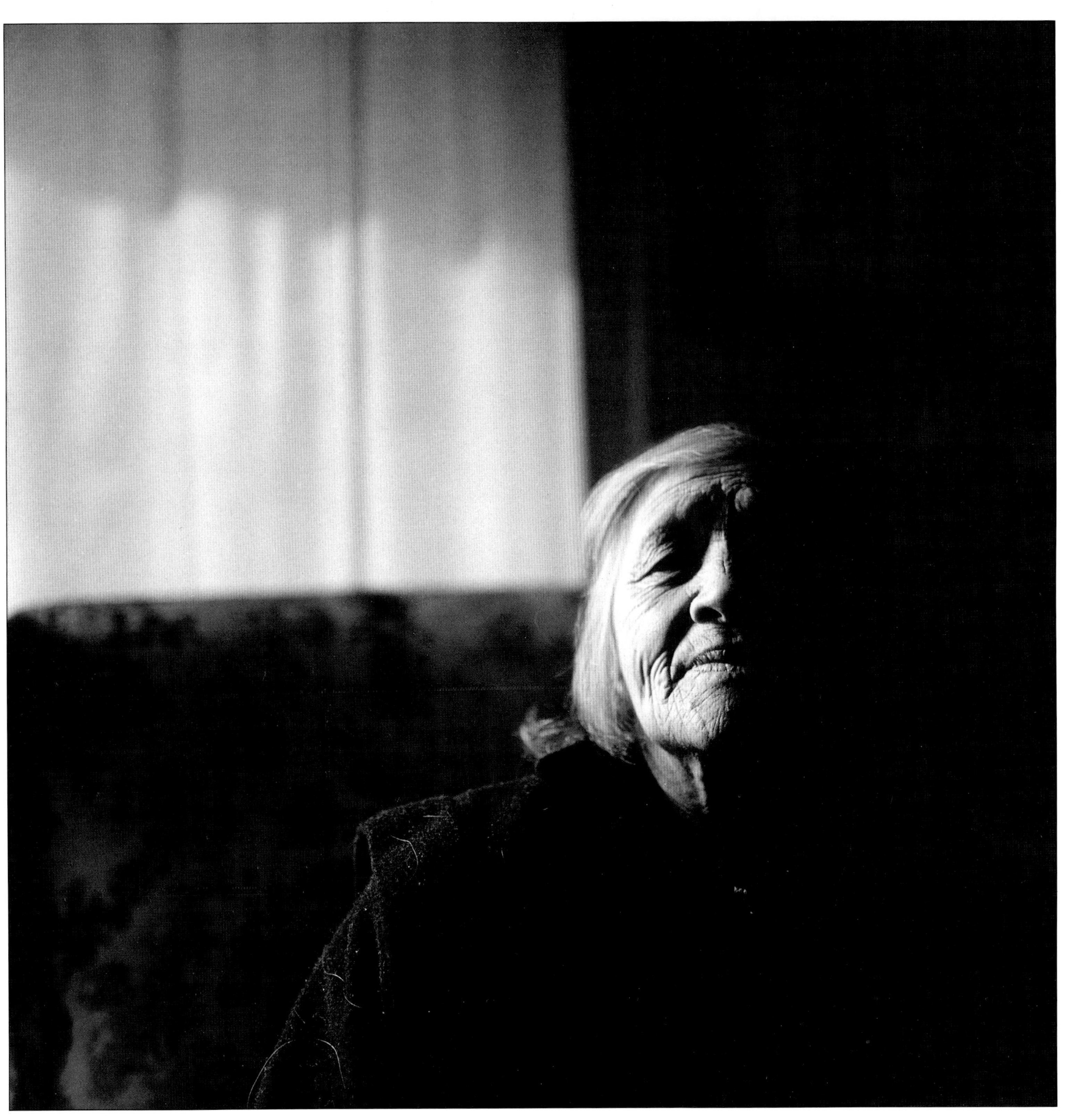

Ruiha Lucy Werahiko

WHIRINAKI

Ko Ngāti Whakaeke me Ngāti Takatoke ngā hapu.
Ko Ngāpuhi te iwi.

I was born on 27 April 1929 to Anihana Ruawhare and Te Rapoti Erueti Heta. In my early years we lived in a nīkau whare on ancestral lands bordering Lake Omāpere, near Kaikohe. My mother kept the whare spotless—if she saw my own place now, she'd have something to say!

When my sisters and I were young—teenagers you'd probably call us now—well, we used to talk about when we'd be married. We liked to think that we would move far away from Lake Omāpere with these husbands we had dreamt up.

Well, when I met Wati Kaio Werahiko, I thought I was marrying a man from Tuwharetoa, because I met him down the line. It turned out he's from the north too!—from Te Hikutu in Whirinaki, in the Hokianga.

I've lived in Whirinaki for forty-four years. Wati and I were married for forty-two of those years, up until his death two years ago.

Over the years I have been influenced not only by the people who are or have been in my life but also by the world of the wairua.

My earliest memory of wairua was when I was eight. I can call it a wairua now, but I can't tell you what it looked like. I just felt its anger.

It happened at the old place at Lake Omāpere. I became sick and couldn't walk.

My mother had a home in Hillcrest Road in Kaikohe at the time, and she took me back there. I remember sitting under the kitchen table in that house, when I saw a man standing in front of me. I could see the Roman sandals on his feet. He asked me, 'What are you doing?' I replied, 'Nothing—I'm sick.' Well, he replied, 'Stand up, little girl'—so I did stand up and walked out from under that table.

Today the inspiration for my role as a kaikaranga comes from that same source—from the wairua that people bring to a place or time. I karakia to the wairua to help me, and to give me strength.

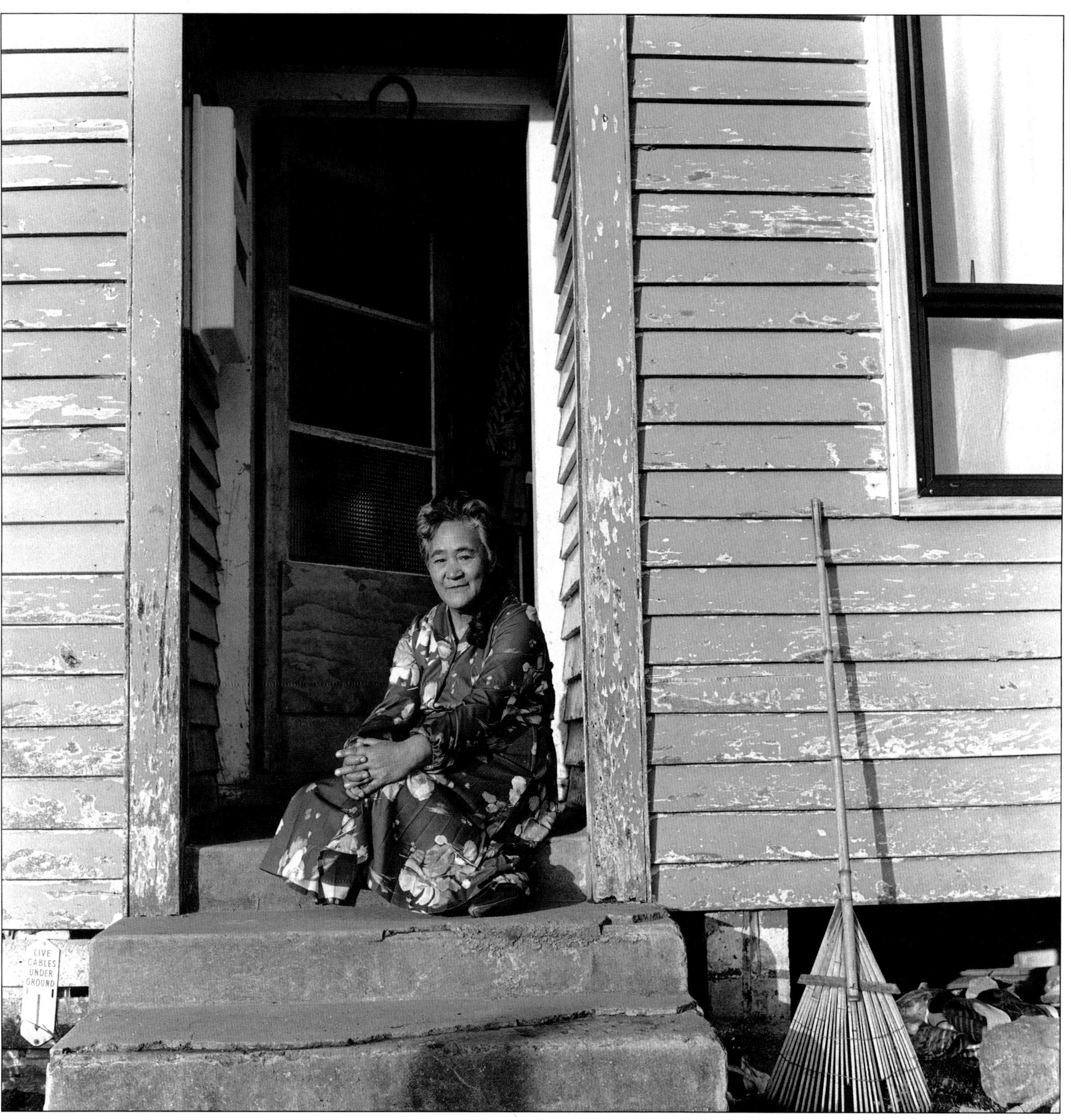
LIVE
CABLES
UNDER
GROUND

Ko Puti Ka Rua Ka Hau Lancaster

KAIKOHE

Ngāti Tuwharetoa me Ngāti Whēuenuku ngā iwi.

Te mihi tuatahi ki to tātou Ariki nāna nei ngā mea katoa. Tēnā hoki te reo tangi o ngā mātua tūpuna e mihi mai nei ki a mātou. Tēnā koutou i ngā tini mate e hinga haere nei i runga i o tātou marae maha o te motu. Nō reira kua tūtaki ngā kōrero kua noho tahi tātou i roto i te rangimarie.

Tēnā koutou, tēnā koutou, tēnā koutou katoa.

With an image it catches a fragment
in the reflection it shows to me
my beauty as a Māori woman
I am living in likeness
of Papatūānuku
for we are interwoven
in this land
we are the carriers of Papatūānuku
As Māori women our beauty and strength
cannot be measured against other cultures
in this land we are
Tangata Whenua
When I am in flight of light
of beauty
it is the heartbeat
of Papatūānuku
I pay heed to
all the dreams
placed inside
the shapes and harmony
of land and sky
Our beauty as Māori Women
we are
He Wāhine
He Taonga

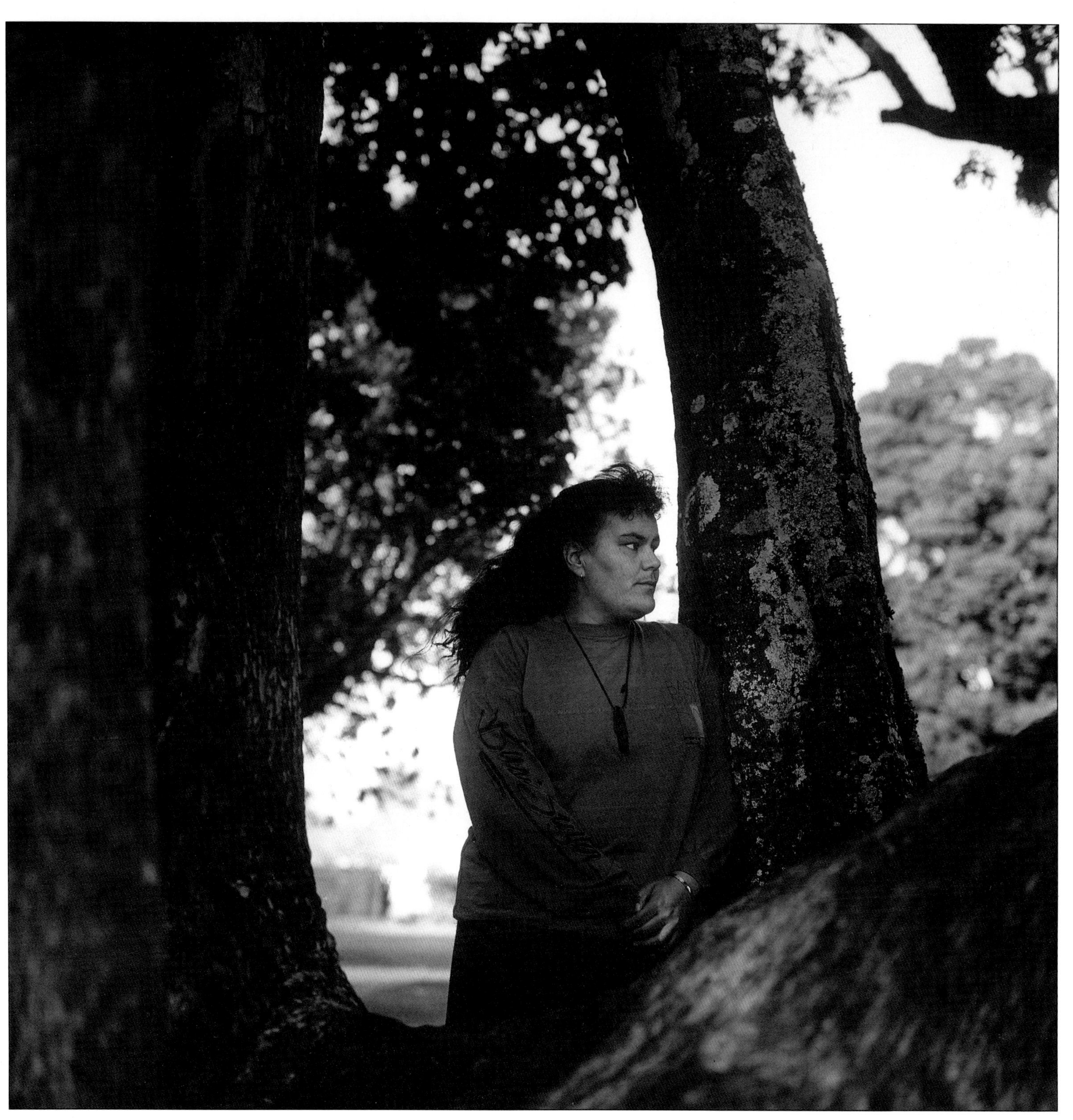

KO PUTI KA RUA KA HAU LANCASTER ▪

Maata Ruwhiu Lawrence

OTAUA

Ko Puhanga Tohorā te maunga.
Ko Pukerata te marae.
Ko Te Rautawanui te whare.
Ko Otaua te kainga.
Ko Ngātokimatawhaorua te waka.
Ko Ngai Tutearu te hapu.
Ko Ngāpuhi te iwi.

He kaiawhina ahau i te marae me te Kohanga Reo o Otaua.
E tekau mā rima āku tamariki, e hia hoki ngā mokopuna.
Tēnā koutou wāhine mā. Tēnā koutou katoa.

Kia ora—greetings to you all.

I am one of the kuia of our marae. The marae is Pukerata. The wharenui is Rautawanui. I am one of the kuia who support the Kohanga Reo in Otaua.

I have fifteen children. I wouldn't be able to tell you how many grandchildren I have.

I support the work of Māori women.

Thank you.

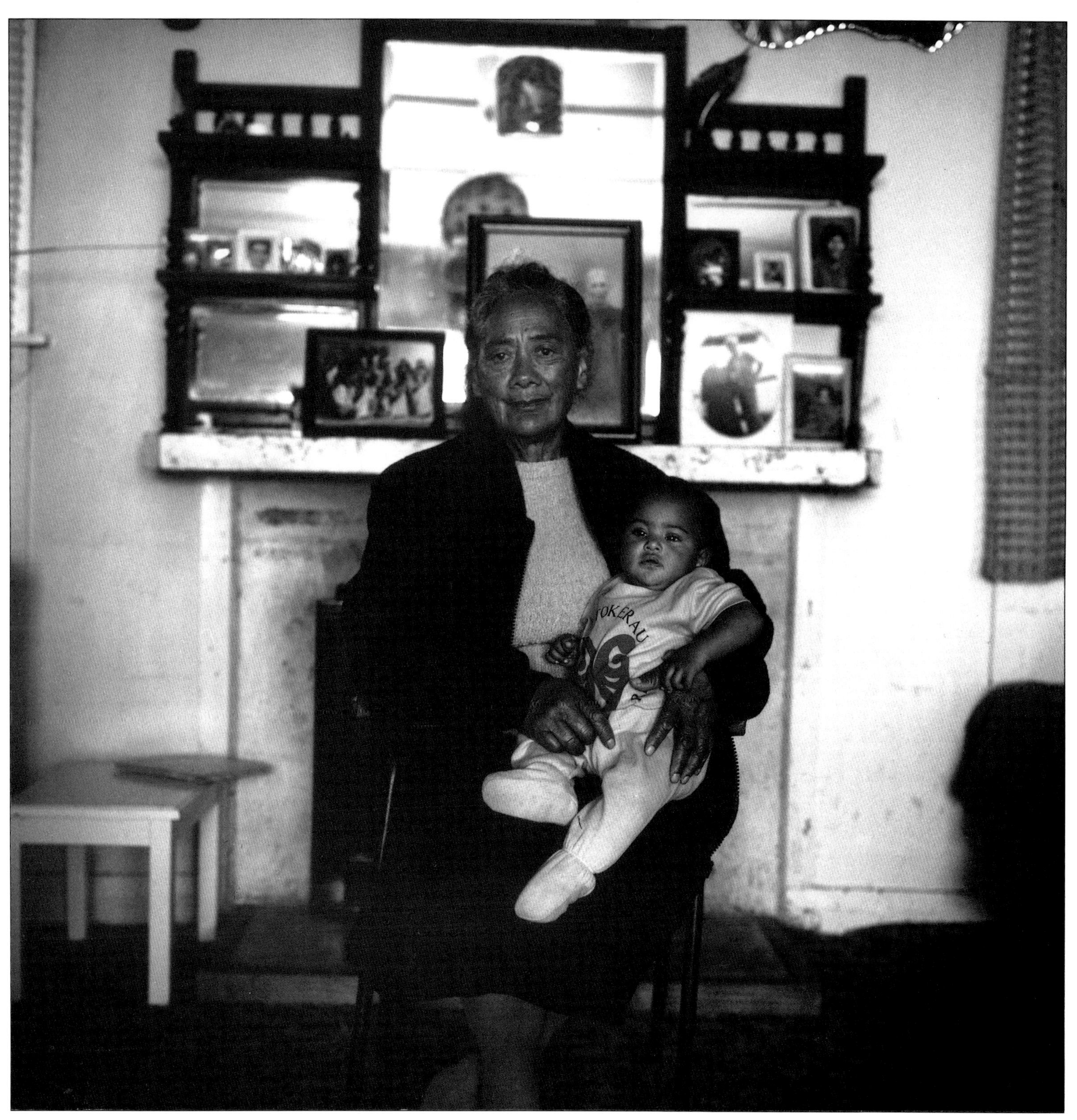
TOKERAU

Molly Walters

WHIRINAKI

Ko Puheke te maunga.
Ko Rangaunu te moana.
Ko Rangi Tane te awa.
Ko Patukoraha te hapu.
Ko Taki Wairua te tangata.
Ko Mamaari te waka.
Ko Ngāti Kahu te iwi.

My father is from Pamapuria, and my mother from Kareponia. I spent my early childhood with my parents at Kareponia, Awanui, in a whānau of nine children. We left home to live in Auckland in 1948, when I was eleven.

Later, having grown up and gone out working, I met my husband, who is of Te Hikutu descent—from Whirinaki in the Hokianga. We had three children and one whāngai, a son. Our youngest daughter died in 1982, at the age of twenty-four, leaving us two sons and one daughter.

My husband and I both worked all our lives at Westfield Freezing Works and Wilson Meats. I would stay home to have my babies and wean them, then my mother looked after the babies while I went back to work.

We both made many friends, and we still get together with some of them to reminisce about old times. When we were younger we always spoke English to each other—that was how we'd been brought up. Now when we're together we all kōrero Māori. At these times I've thought, 'Here we are now—all elders of our families and in our communities, but boy did we have some fun when we were younger.' I think the memories of my own youth help me to understand the young people of today.

We came home to my husband's people to live in 1985. Really the death of our daughter in 1982 brought us back. Now when I look back I think it was material things that kept me in Auckland, and I have had to come back here to Whirinaki to find the important things in life for me—like my reo. Now I've got time to speak Māori with all my mokopuna.

We have eighteen grandchildren and three great-grandchildren, and we are kaumātua and kuia for Opononi Area School and for Pa Te Aroha Marae in Whirinaki, Hokianga.

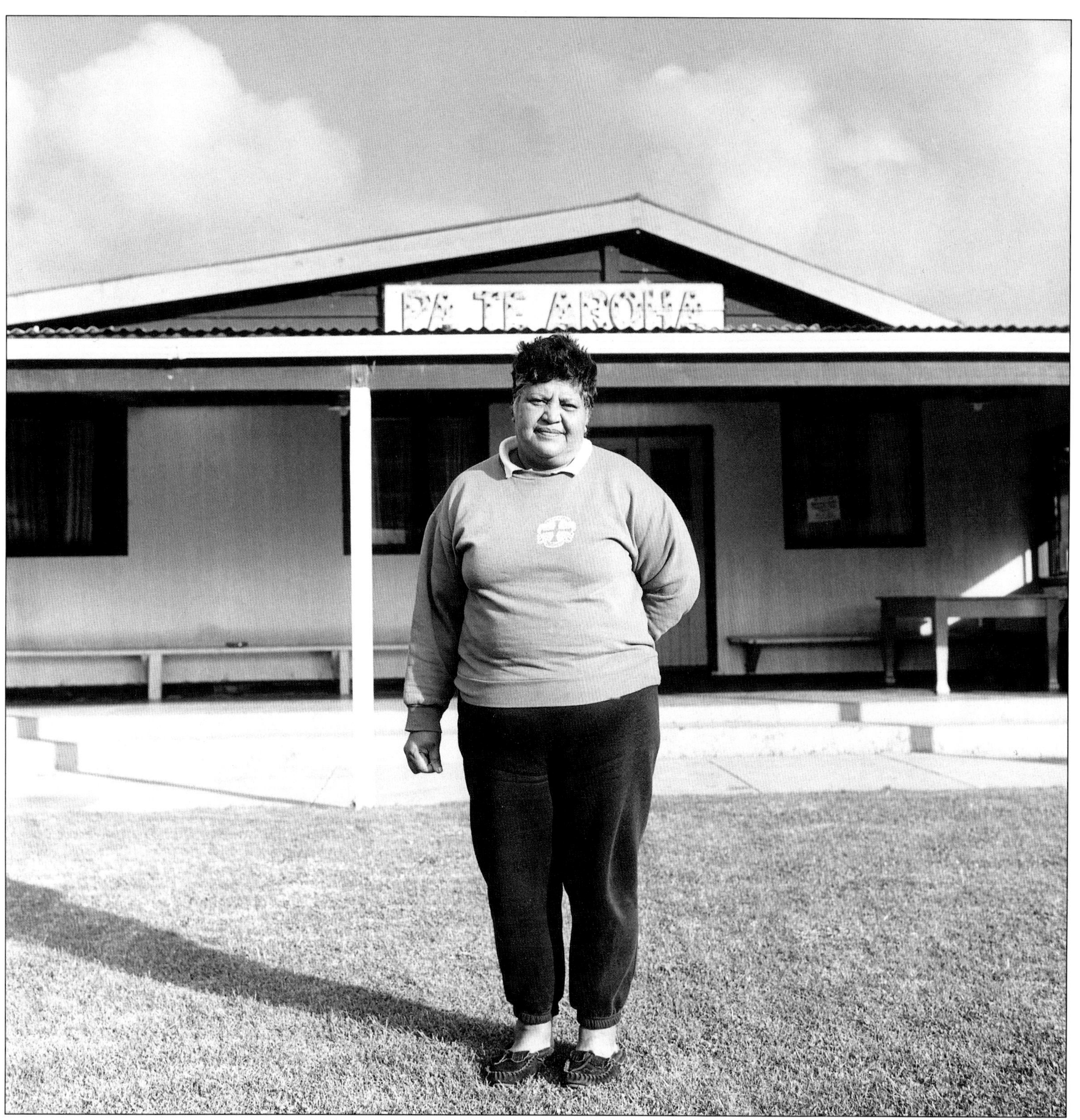
PA TE AROHA

Ada Aroha Patuwai

MATARĀUA

Ko Ngāpuhi, ko Mahurehure ngā iwi.
Ko Patukeha te hapu.

I'm from the Bay of Islands, though I was born and grew up in Whangarei, where I went to Whangarei Girls High School.

I gained a lot of experience meeting people, learning skills, and eventually gaining employment through my involvement with the Latter Day Saints.

While living in Wellington I met and married Glen, who is from Ngāti Porou, Gisborne.

We travelled north to Matarāua with our daughter, Kelly. The idea was just to visit Mum, have a change of scenery, and take a rest. To my surprise I realised I had been here for three months already, and had no desire to go back to the city.

We were a young family, with little knowledge of our Māoritanga, although it was part of my teachings as a child.

We settled into a whānau home, and I enrolled Kelly in a bilingual class at the Kaikohe West School, and our son, Iraia, in Kohanga Reo to give them exposure to their reo. My tamariki have learned to waiata Māori and kōrero Māori every day.

We have lived below Ngai-ta-wake Marae for five years. It's great when the marae is open, because plenty can be learnt. The whare was once just a church building left on site, and is now being slowly restored by the local people on Employment Services courses and working bees. The people are building a wharekai, gardening and weaving, and there are still more crafts and skills to be learnt.

We've been here eight years, and we now have three children. In this valley, we live in a community of many relations who have strong ties to family and cultural traditions.

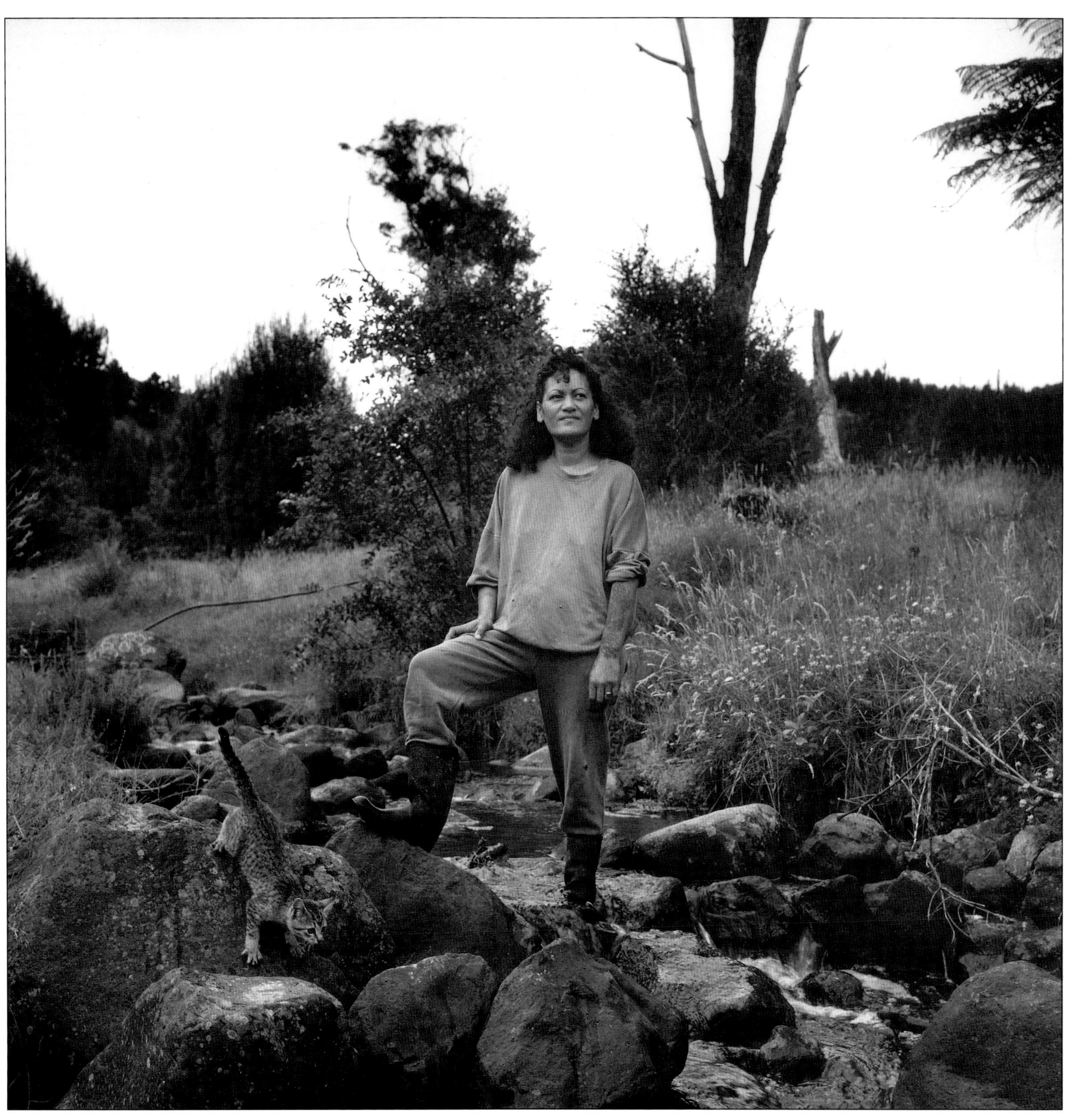

ADA AROHA PATUWAI ▪

Hera Kopa

OTAUA

Kia ora. I live in a little community called Otaua, situated in the Hokianga, North Island.

I am involved with the Otaua Te Kohanga Reo, having three children there myself. I also, as a young parent, support Te Kura Kaupapa Māori, as I have one tamaiti going there too. Te Kura Kaupapa Māori will be the future for the rest of my tamariki as well.

My aim is for my tamariki to learn their reo, and as they get older they will know their own tongue, as I myself am also learning. As it has already been said, te reo starts at home, at the learning age.

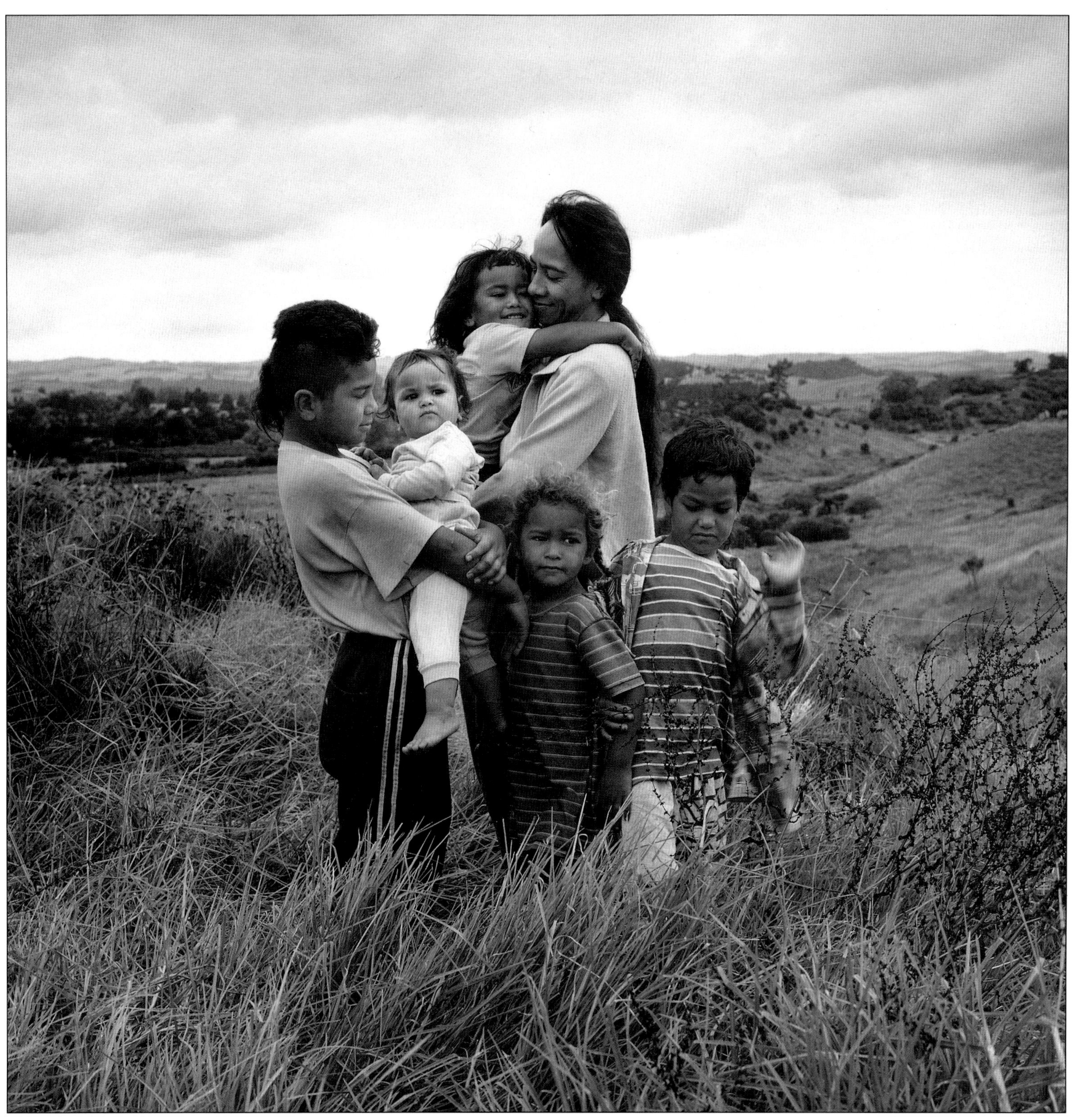

Annais Allen

OPONONI

My mother is Ngawini Komene of Ngāti Rahiri/Ngāti Kawa and Te Uri o Hua, and my father is Marsh Allen (Napia) of Ngai-ta-wake-ki-te-tua-whenua and Ngāti Rēhia.

Right now I am hapu with my first child. I know there are responsibilities of memory and of people and places that I have, as a mother and as a Māori woman, to give to this child. I have realised that one of these really important memories is that my parents gave to me the basis of knowing who I am, and where I come from.

For as long as I can remember, my parents told me, and my sisters and brothers, stories of our ancestors and their ancestral lands, seas, sacred mountains and rivers. We were often taken to these places as children to play, observe, or participate in whatever activity was taking place. Always these places and people are in my consciousness.

Being able to align myself with hapu, lands, rivers, seas, and marae means for me that regardless of however many times land ownership may change in today's legal systems, and wherever I may choose to live, I shall always belong to the land. No legal system can tell me that I do not.

I have two birth sisters, two birth brothers, many, many whānau sisters, and not so many whānau brothers! They come from many parts of Aotearoa and the world; some are Māori, and some are not. I consider that my family is not only those related to me by birth, but that my family can in fact also be based upon caring, nurturing, and common interests—dare I say even upon love for others!

Responsibility takes many shapes. I enjoy the tools of creativity—like thinking, writing, painting, being in business, finance, and birthing. They give form to the experiences and ideas that are my responsibility to share.

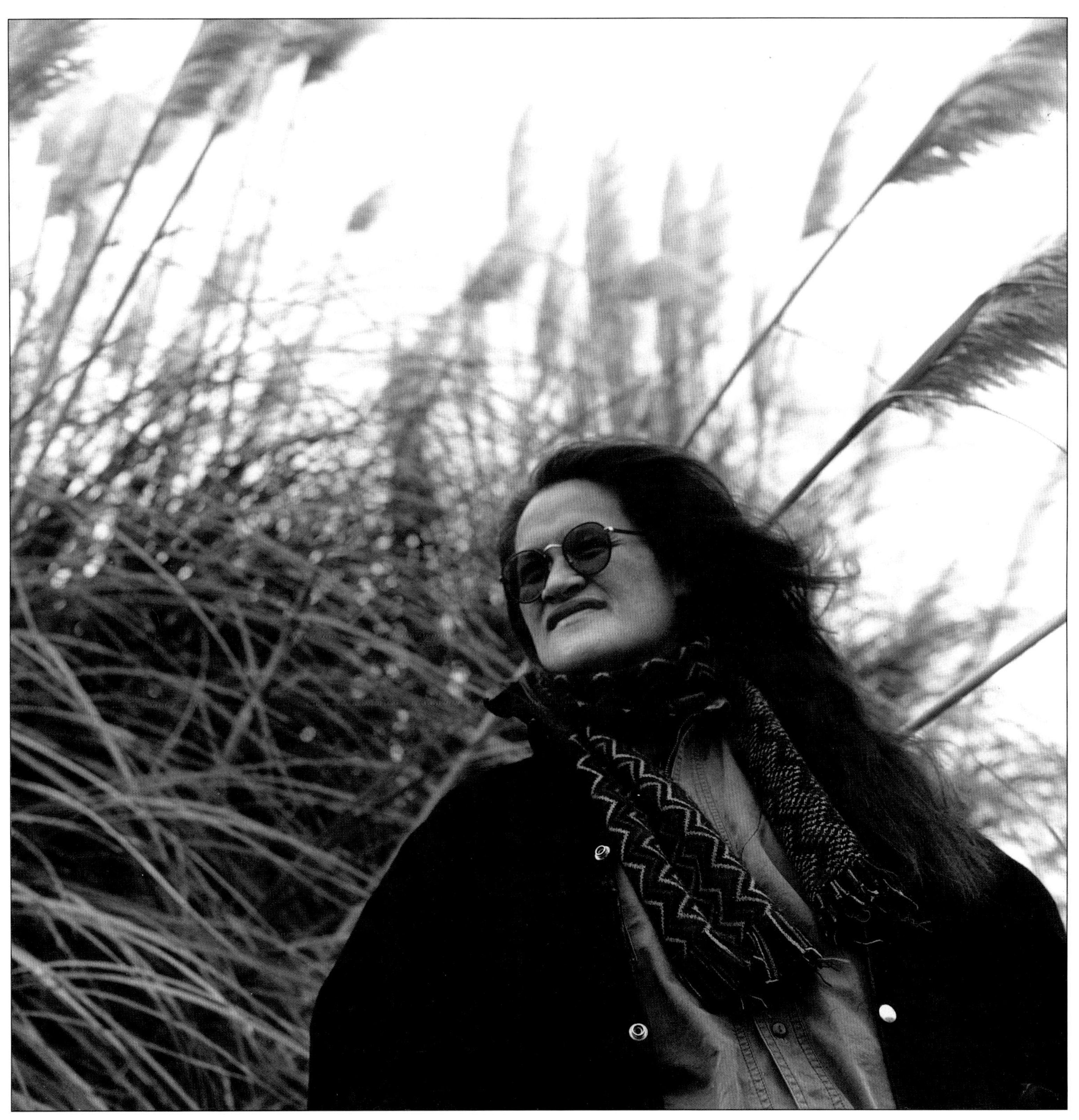

Helene Leaf

WHIRINAKI

Ko Ngāpuhi te iwi.
Ko Hikutu te hapu.
Ko Ngātokimatawhaorua te waka.
Ko Whirinaki te awa.
Ko Te Ramaroa te maunga.

I was born at the end of the last world war, in Hokianga. My parents are still both living in Whirinaki in the Hokianga, and I count this as a great blessing.

My mother comes from Nelson, where her family were involved in publishing and education. My father is of Te Hikutu hapu.

Being Māori was difficult in my early years; however, I was taught well and believed that I could do anything.

I had a wonderful childhood, with many, many hours of adventure and challenge—swimming, riding horses, hunting and fishing.

While very young we all learnt to be responsible, to accept the consequences of our actions, and to sort out whatever situation we found ourselves in.

At school I excelled only in physical activities.

While people's expectations of me have often been low, I am stubborn: if I was told I wouldn't be able to do something, I would set out to prove people wrong.

Of all the things I've achieved, I consider the most important one is the rearing of my eight tamariki. They are bicultural and bilingual. My strength as a Māori woman has been their strength, and my pride theirs.

When all our tamariki are able to develop a strong identity and an awareness of each other's culture, then we will be a proud people in a diverse and rich country.

Tama tū, tama ora; tama noho, tama mate.

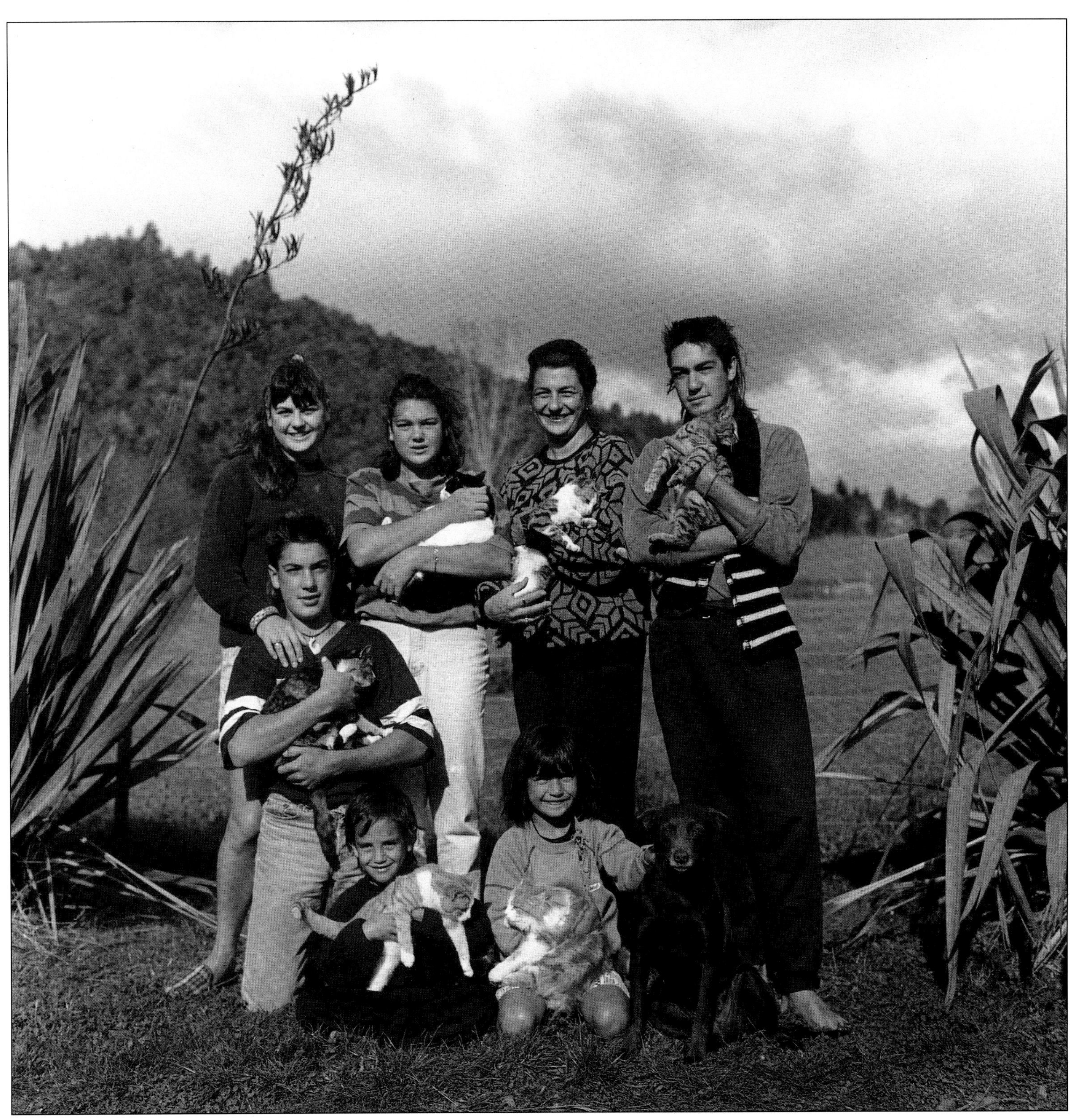

Kath Kopa

OTAUA

Kia ora wāhine mā.

First—my whakapapa comes from the seven canoes: Tainui, Kurahaupo, Te Arawa, Tokomaru, Takitimu, Aotea, Mataatua. Because of this, I believe that I am a unique Māori woman, and am very proud of my ancestry.

My kainga noho is Otaua. It is a little place in the Hokianga. We have a maunga that's part of the history of Ngāpuhi, that people called Puhanga Tohorā.

Ko Kath Kopa tōkū ingoa. Ko Whetu Kopa tōkū hoa tāne. We have six children—their names are: Jennifer Kahu, Hana, Hera, Erihapeti, Takapari, Tupuarangi—and seventeen mokopuna. The eldest mokopuna is fourteen years old and the youngest is six months.

My mahi in the community ranges from, first, Kohanga Reo (learning nest) to Kura Kaupapa Māori (Māori school of learning), Te Korowai Aroha (Māori marriage guidance), Te Kupenga o te Ora (Māori women's group), Te Ara Tapu o Te Wharetangata (cervical cancer), School Board of Trustees, Care and Protection for Children panel, voluntary iwi community work and being a supportive person in counselling groups. All this is a meaningful challenge for me.

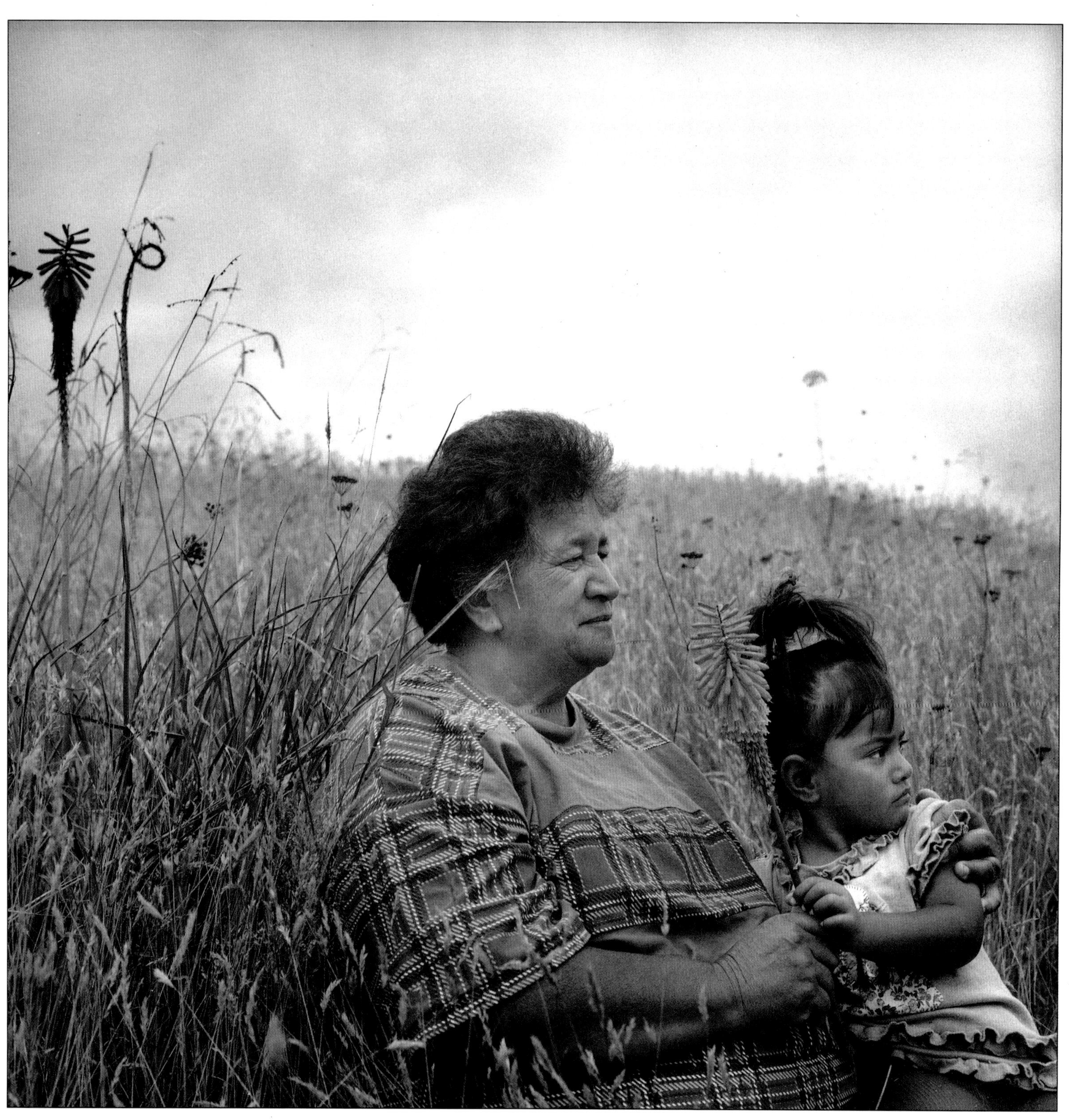

Mavis Meteria Hepi-Heremaia

TAHEKE

Ko Ngāpuhi te iwi.
Ko Ngāti Kuta te hapu.
Ko Ngāti Wai te hapu.

I am currently co-ordinating a programme for Māori couples in relationship issues. This programme is done in a Māori way, for Māori and by Māori, with Te Korowai Aroha of Ngāpuhi.

I firmly believe in leading by example.

I am a mother of three teenage children and work closely with Māori women, in the areas of self-esteem, confidence and support, and abuse counselling.

My one regret is that of missing out on my reo, and believe this is due mainly to my parents not feeling confident about speaking Māori to us because it was forbidden at school.

My experiences of trying to learn Māori are many. I have found a way, and that is to visit the marae and listen to the kōrero, as much is repeated. This helps me to become familiar with the words.

I sincerely hope that the few hints I have given may be of help to other Māori women who are having problems in any one of these areas.

Nō reira e wāhine mā, kia kaha.

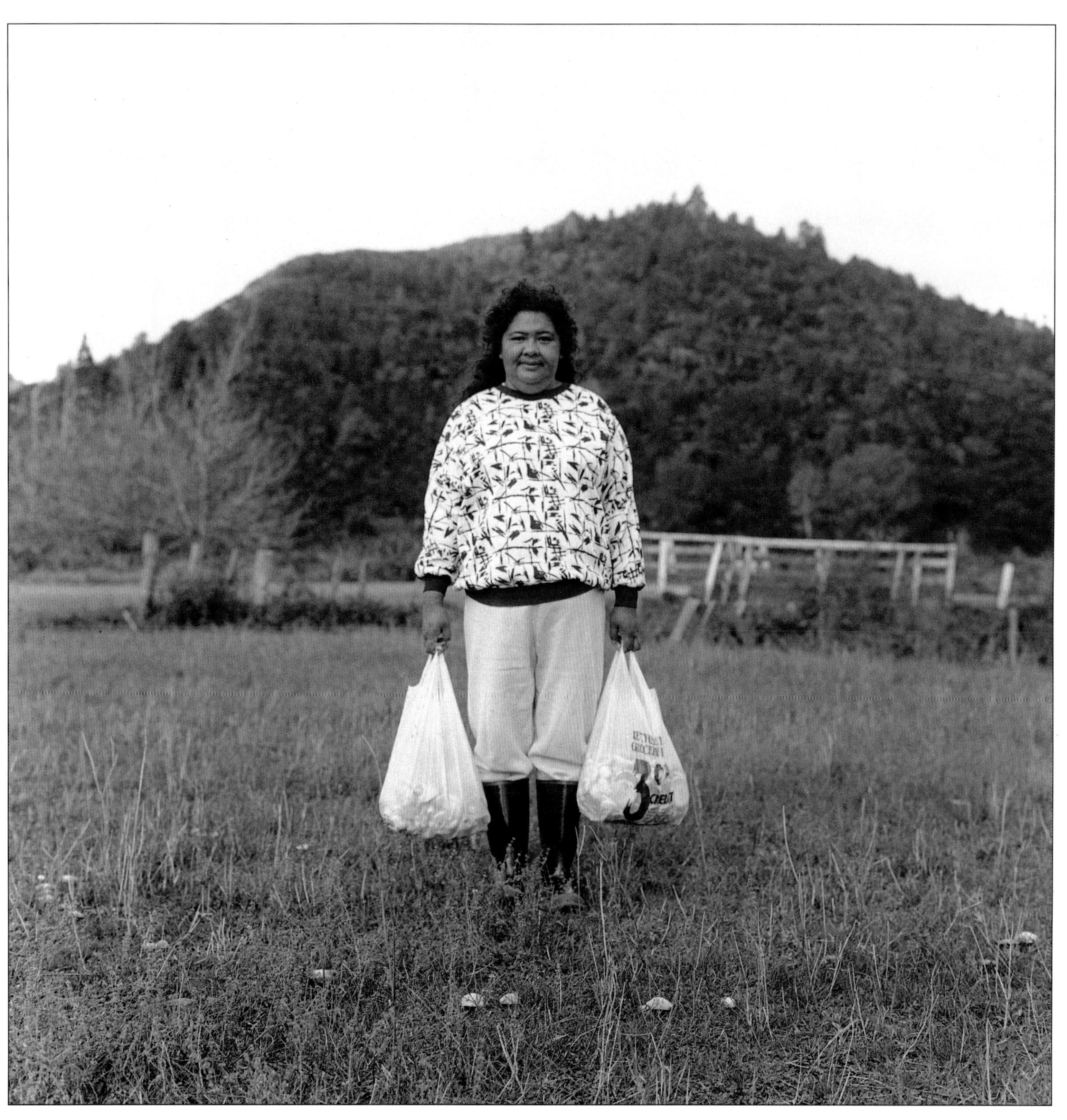

MAVIS METERIA HEPI-HEREMAIA ▪

Joy Ngaropo-Hau

KAIKOHE

Ko Panguru te maunga tapu.
Ko Waihou te awa me te marae.
Ko Waimirirangi te whare tupuna.
Ko Pare-puna-o-te-ora te whare manaaki i te iwi.
I te taha o tōku matua ko Kai Tutae, ko Wae Koi
me Ngāti Te Reinga ngā hapu.
I te taha o tōku whaea ko Ngāti Korokoro te hapu.
Ko Te Rarawa ki Hokianga te iwi.
Ko Hokianga te moana.
Ko Ngātokimatawhaorua me Mamaari ngā waka.
Ko Te Wano rāua ko Merepaea Ngaropo ōku mātua.

Tekau ngā tamariki i roto i tōku whānau. I tupu ake mātou i roto o Waihou, Panguru. I kura mātou ki te kura Katorika o Panguru. Ko tōku tuakana me tētahi o ōku tungane i waimarie ka haere rāua ki ngā kura Katorika o Hato Hohepa me Hato Petera. I taua wā kāhore o mātou kura tuarua, ēngari i e tau kotahi mano iwa rau, ono tekau mā rua, ka hanga he kura tuarua ki tō mātou nei takiwā. Ka kura tonu mātou i te kainga, nō taku hāunga atu ki te karaehe tuaono ka haere ahau ki te kura mo ngā kōtiro o Tamaki Makaurau.

Nō taku mutunga i te kura ka haere ahau ki te mahi nāhi i te hōhipere o Akarana. He maha ngā mahi i taua wā.

I ahau e takakau ana ka nuku māua ko tōku hoa a Tihi Puanaki ki Otautahi—Te Waipounamu. I reira ka tutaki ahau ki tōku hoa rangatira a Rūroa—Lu Mokau Hau. Tokowhā a māua tamariki, ko Marino, ko Te Kaiarahi (Kaihui), Ana me Te Ao Marama. Ināianei kua hoki mai mātou ki te hau kainga.

Kia ora koutou katoa.

Ko te tīmatanga o te mātauranga
Ko te wēhi ki te Atua
Te tīmatanga me te whakamutunga o ngā mea katoa.

Tēnā koutou, tēnā koutou, tēnā rā koutou katoa.

Lu and I met through our respect and love for traditional performing arts and culture. Over the years we have belonged to kapa haka groups as teachers, as well as performing competitively and for pure entertainment.

Like Lu and I, our four tamariki have always been influenced by te reo me ngā tikanga Māori. It is all around us, in the life that we have as a family.

As parents and as teachers we make great efforts to find ways and approaches to learning that arouse, motivate and uplift the minds of all the tamariki with whom we are regularly in contact.

Many people have played a big part in shaping our lives into what we are today—our parents, our tūpuna—many many people. It is from these people that we have learnt that it is our responsibility as Māori and as adults to ensure that all our tamariki understand and acknowledge the strength of their own culture first.

Our culture is positive and powerful. Our people would ask you, 'What is the greatest thing (in this world)?' And their response would be, 'It is people, it is people, it is people!'

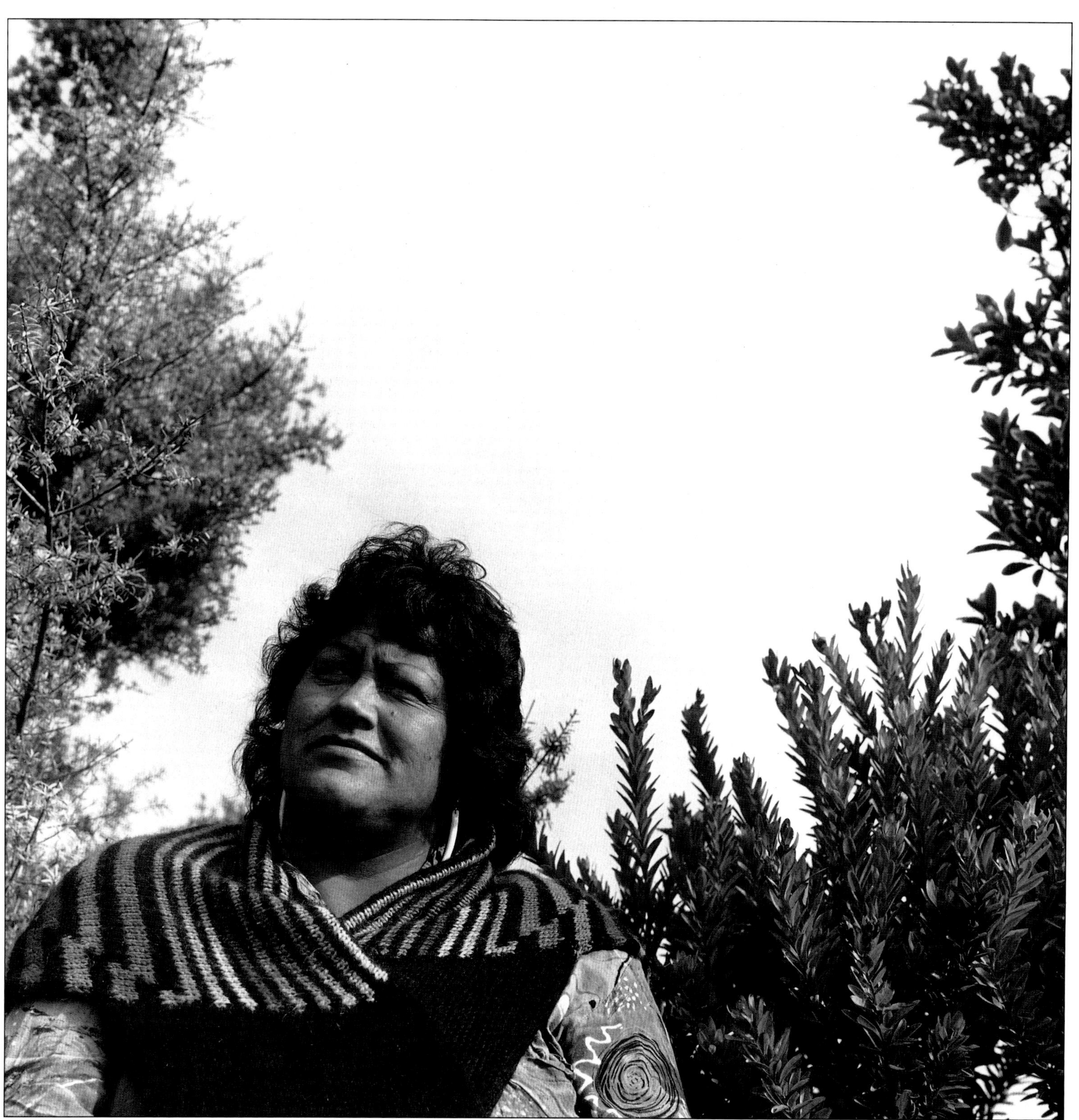

Nicole Presland

WHIRINAKI

Ko Te Ramaroa te maunga.
Ko Whirinaki te awa.
Ko Ngātokimatawhaorua te waka.
Ko Te Hikutu te hapu.
Ko Ngāpuhi te iwi.

I am a descendant of the Leafs from Whirinaki. Having been brought up in Auckland, I am eternally grateful to have my whānau in the Hokianga, as their support and knowledge has strengthened my identity, and I have gained confidence and a strong sense of pride through this.

I perceive Māori women to be pillars of strength, beauty and knowledge—this shines through above all else. Amongst other young Māori women I see a need for a continuance of this strength and an accessible well to draw it from. This for many is hard to get when they are caught up and isolated in city life.

The position of Māori women in our society, the way they are sometimes not given the acknowledgement and support they deserve, leads me to despair, but change is continuous, and eternity is a long time.

I sometimes look for someone to thank—for my life and for who I am. At these times I turn to my tūpuna, for without them, I would not exist at all.

Nō reira—kia kaha wāhine mā.
Kia ora koutou katoa.

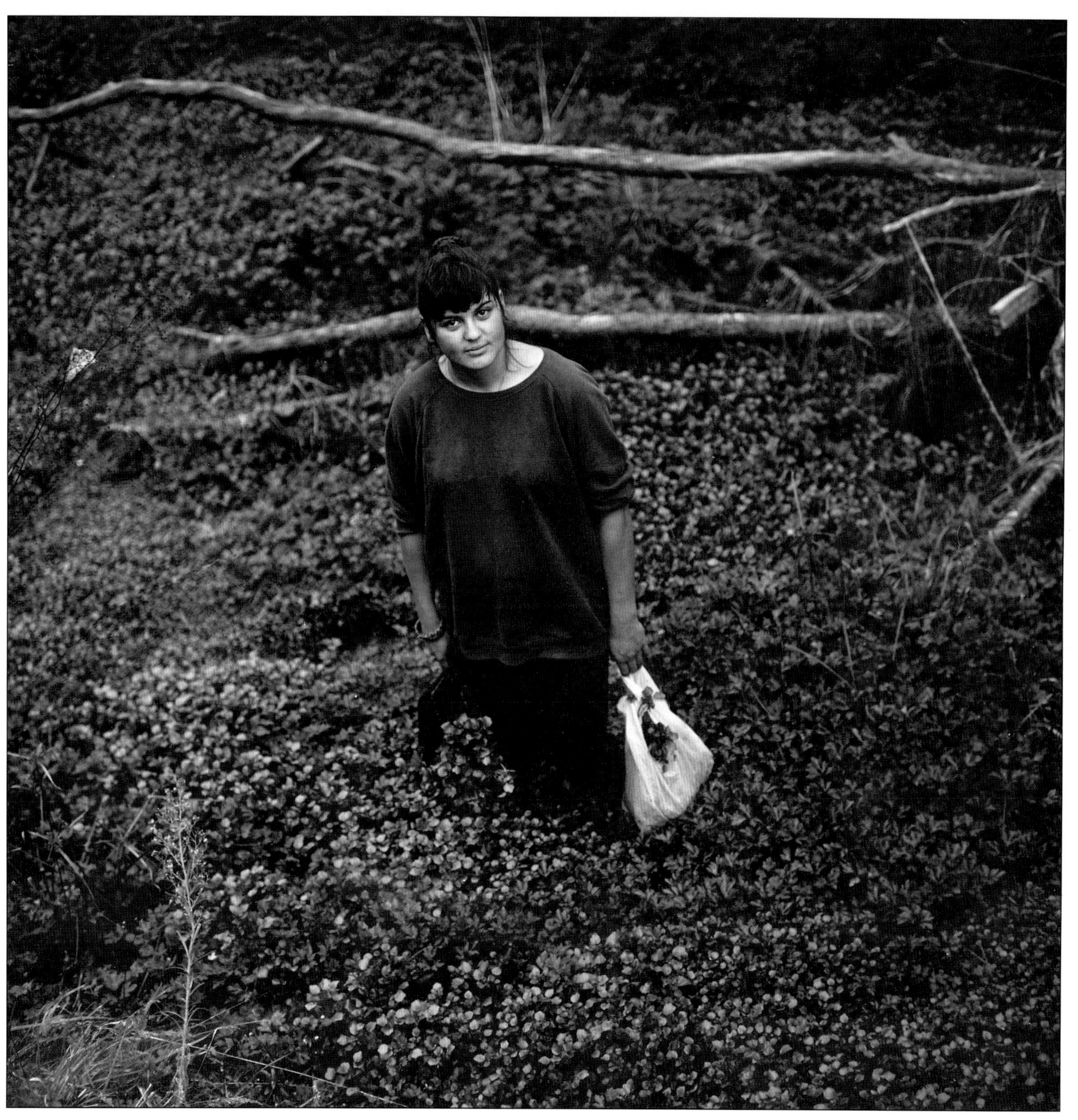